W9-BNF-649

New Dimensions
of Political
Economy

New Dimensions of Political Economy

BY WALTER W. HELLER

NEW YORK

W · W · NORTON & COMPANY · INC ·

COPYRIGHT © 1967, 1966 BY

THE PRESIDENT & FELLOWS OF HARVARD COLLEGE

Published by W. W. Norton & Company, Inc., 55 Fifth Avenue, New York 10003, by arrangement with Harvard University Press

Library of Congress Catalog Card No. 67-21740

ALL RIGHTS RESERVED

Published simultaneously in Canada by George J. McLeod Limited, Toronto

The Godkin Lectures at Harvard University 1966
The Godkin Lectures on the Essentials of Free Government and the Duties of the Citizen were established at Harvard University in 1903 in memory of Edwin Lawrence Godkin (1831-1902)
They are given annually under the auspices of the Harvard Graduate School of Public Administration

PRINTED IN THE UNITED STATES OF AMERICA

2 3 4 5 6 7 8 9 0

TO MY WIFE

Contents

Preface to the Paperbound Edition

As the U.S. economy undergoes the buffeting of war in Vietnam and looks hopefully toward the problems of peace, the "new economics" is being put to a series of stern tests.

First, after escalation in Vietnam turned the record peacetime expansion of 1961-1965 into the over-expansion of 1965-1966, could economic policy hold inflation in check without direct controls? The answer: it did, but it could and should have done better. Inflation was held to less than a 3 percent annual rate for the eighteen months after escalation began in mid-1965. But had the policy process delivered a stronger dose of taxes instead of an overdose of tight money, inflation would have been milder and the economy would have been in better balance.

Second, as expansion entered its seventh year early in 1967, it looked a bit tired and drawn. Excess inventories, depressed housing, hesitant consumers, and an ebbing investment boom seemed to require thinking about the unthinkable: war and recession side by side. Could economic policy be nimble and selective enough to keep total demand moving up while restoring balance to the economy?

Third, an end to war in Vietnam would present new problems of economic transition and open new opportunities for economic betterment. Would the "new economics" succeed in minimizing the problems and maximizing the opportunities?

Grounds for optimism in answering these questions will be found in this book, especially in its development of the theme that modern economic intelligence and advice have been woven into the everyday fabric of White House decision-making — for good.

One's optimism is strengthened by the flexible and responsive adaptation of policy to economic change in the months since this book was written. For example:

- The suspension of the investment credit in 1966 — late, but still helpful — and its quick restoration in 1967.

- The flexibility-in-reserve of the proposed 6 percent income-tax surcharge, which could be postponed, cut back, or cancelled in response to economic developments.

- The new tone of Congressional economic thinking, reflected in statements by both Republican and Democratic leaders, that the fate of the surcharge hangs on the state of the economy (rather than the state of the budget).

- The impounding, by the President, of appropriated funds for highways and other purposes in the face of overheating in 1966 followed by the progressive release of funds in a cooling economy in 1967.

- The Federal Reserve Board's resolute policy of monetary ease in 1967, responding as it should to the sluggish pace of this year's demand and production rather than to the cost-push echoes of last year's excessive demand.

- President Johnson's call (in his January 1967 Economic Report) for a "major and coordinated effort to review our readiness" for a smooth economic readjustment after the war in Vietnam ends, using such instruments as tax cuts, easier money, expansion of high-priority expenditure programs, and enlarged federal support to state and local governments.

Even as we meet the problems of economic softness in 1967 and of economic transition after Vietnam, we need to remind ourselves that ending the waste of unemployment and slow growth is only part — albeit a large part — of the battle. Modern economic policy, both here and abroad, has yet to demonstrate that it can deliver full employment and vigorous growth and at the same time maintain, in a free economy, reasonable price stability and balance-of-payments equilibrium. That capstone of the "new economics" is still being formed.

W. W. H.

Minneapolis, Minnesota
April 3, 1967

Preface

In the title of this book I use the term "political economy" advisedly. For the new dimensions I explore in these pages are chiefly in the *uses* of economics rather than the *substance*. Today's talk of an "intellectual revolution" and a "new economics" arises not out of startling discoveries of new economic truths but out of the swift and progressive weaving of modern economics into the fabric of national thinking and policy.

This process of rapid change has thrust the political economist into a new, more responsible — and more exposed — role as Presidential adviser and consensus-seeker. It has greatly broadened the uses of economics — and economists — by Presidents. In the first chapter, I examine that new role and those broader uses and their implications, emphasizing not only the emergence of Presidents Kennedy and Johnson as practicing economists, but the patterns they seem to have set for the future.

Change has brought a new look not just to economic process but to economic policy. Gone is the countercyclical syndrome of the 1950's. Policy now centers on gap closing and growth, on realizing and enlarging the economy's noninflationary potential. The second chapter deals with the nature of this shift, with yesterday's pleasures of expansion, today's pangs of inflation, and tomorrow's promises of fiscal abundance.

Among the most exciting of these promises is the forging of a stronger fiscal base for our federalism, not only by expanding our system of Federal aid, but — when the demands of Vietnam relent — by developing new forms of fiscal support for state and local government. The fiscal challenge of federalism and our new opportunities for coping with it are the subject of the final chapter.

I am indebted to the Ford Foundation for the fellowship that gave me the time to do much of the underlying work for this book. And I am grateful to George L. Perry, L. L. Ecker-Racz, Arthur Okun, and Joseph A. Pechman for their constructive criticism of the manuscript. This book is an expansion of the Godkin Lectures which I was privileged to give at Harvard University in March 1966.

Walter W. Heller

August 27, 1966
Minneapolis, Minnesota

New Dimensions
of Political
Economy

§ CHAPTER I § Advice and Consensus in Economic Policy Making

Economics has come of age in the 1960's. Two Presidents have recognized and drawn on modern economics as a source of national strength and Presidential power. Their willingness to use, for the first time, the full range of modern economic tools underlies the unbroken U.S. expansion since early 1961 — an expansion that in its first five years created over seven million new jobs, doubled profits, increased the nation's real output by a third, and closed the $50-billion gap between actual and potential production that plagued the American economy in 1961.

Together with the gradual closing of that huge production gap has come — part as cause, part as consequence — a gradual, then rapid, narrowing of the intellectual gap between professional economists and men of affairs, between economic advisers and decision makers. The paralyzing grip of economic myth and false fears on policy has been loosened, perhaps even broken. We at last accept in fact what was accepted in law twenty years ago (in the

Employment Act of 1946), namely, that the Federal government has an overarching responsibility for the nation's economic stability and growth.[1] And we have at last unleashed fiscal and monetary policy for the aggressive pursuit of those objectives.

These are profound changes. What they have wrought is not the creation of a "new economics," but the completion of the Keynesian Revolution — thirty years after John Maynard Keynes fired the opening salvo. And they have put the political economist at the President's elbow.

THE AGE OF THE ECONOMIST

The economist "arrived" on the New Frontier and is firmly entrenched in the Great Society. Indeed, the worst fears of those who dread the Age of the Economist are confirmed by the list of professional economists currently or recently serving in high places: directors of the Budget Bureau and the Agency for International Development; ambassadors; key policy makers in the White House and the Pentagon; under secretaries of State, Treasury, and Agriculture; Federal Reserve Board presidents and members; and, not surprisingly, a long list of members of the Council of Economic Advisers (CEA).

President Johnson underscored his esteem of economists at the swearing-in of a new CEA member early in 1966.

He described the occasion as "a bit of barter with Harvard University. Harvard made us give them back Otto Eckstein. We wouldn't do it until they gave us Jim Duesenberry."

He went on: "Dr. Duesenberry, as we all know, is one of this Nation's leading economists. When I was growing up, that didn't seem to mean very much, but since I grew up we have learned the error of our ways."

He predicted that the new Council member would "write a record here, as his colleagues . . . have written, that will excite the admiration of not only all their fellow Americans, but will excite the admiration of leaders in other governments throughout the world who frequently comment to me about the wisdom, the foresight, the stability of the United States of America and its policies." [2]

Interwoven with the growing Presidential reliance on economists has been a growing political and popular belief that modern economics can, after all, deliver the goods — that even if they never meet a payroll or carry a precinct, economists who can meet a crisis and help carry an expansion into its sixth year may still be worth their salt. As *Business Week* put it, the record of five years of "remarkable growth — and remarkable stability — in the U.S. economy . . . has raised the prestige of economists — especially those who espouse the so-called new economics — to an all-time high." [3]

How did economists come to positions of such power and prestige? And are they there to stay? In part, we must seek the answer in the internal advances of recent decades in positive economics, in the economic knowledge — the theory, analysis, facts, and figures — on which policy must be based. But in equal or greater measure, the answer lies in the external advances of recent years in the uses of normative economics, in the conscious pursuit of national goals through economic policy, especially by Presidents.

INTERNAL FORCES

At the root of the recent revolution in economic policy and ideology lie three decades of progress in economic science, highlighted by

• Lord Keynes' spectacular rescue (via the *General Theory of Employment, Interest, and Money* in 1936) of economics from the wilderness of classical equilibrium which had assumed away the critical issues of employment and income levels and their determinants;

• Alvin Hansen's Americanization of Keynes, which put a translated and enhanced *General Theory* at the disposal of a whole new generation of economists in this country;

• Simon Kuznets' seminal work on the concepts of national income and gross national product (GNP), which the U.S. Department of Commerce translated into annual national income estimates by 1934 and GNP estimates by 1942 (adding quarterly estimates in 1947);

• Paul Samuelson's "neoclassical synthesis," which ranges the contributions of the classical economist side-by-side with those of Keynes in balanced policy for full employment and efficient resource allocation;

• The contributions of a new generation of computer-oriented economists, whose quantitative work is increasing the scope and reliability of economic analysis and forecasting.

Part of the political economist's strength, then, lies in an ever-broadening base of economic theory, statistics, and research. But his influence with decision makers — whether in the White House or in the Pentagon — also derives from his particular analytical approach. Problems of choice are his meat and drink. His method is to factor out the costs, the benefits, and the net advantage or disadvantage of alternative courses of action. Where possible, he does so in quantitative terms. Where not, he substitutes qualitative appraisals of the likely effects of given actions. In either case, his approach is to define problems and cast up solutions in terms that clearly tell the decision maker how he can serve one objective at minimum cost to others, for example, how he can serve the ends of full employment or high growth at minimum cost to price stability and the balance of trade.[4]

Put differently, the political economist typically thinks in terms of trade-offs — for example, the trade-off between jobs and inflation, the problem at which we pitch our Phillips Curves (relating the behavior of prices to the behavior of unemployment); the trade-off between international payments equilibrium and internal expansion, for which monetary policy did the "twist" (pushing short-term interest rates up to discourage the outflow of volatile funds, while holding long-term rates down to encourage capital spending); the trade-off between price-wage stability and unfettered markets, for which we erected the wage-price guideposts (providing guides to noninflationary wage and price behavior).

Further, the economist's discipline constantly conditions him to marginal rather than all-or-nothing thinking, to a balancing of costs and benefits at the margins of policy adjustment. And more and more, in recent years, he has introduced uncertainty and probability into his dynamic models and analysis. Trade-offs, marginal adjustments, uncertainty, probability — small wonder that the economist finds a ready home, and finds himself *at* home, in the governmental decision-making process.

Suppose the problem before him, in an economy overheated by the demands of the war in Vietnam, is to take some of the inflationary steam out of private spending on plant and equipment. In defining the problem, he will already have measured the probable costs of inaction: (1) rising prices, intensified labor shortages, and growing delivery lags in machinery, equipment, and construction; (2) reinforcement of wage demands, leading to increases in unit labor costs; (3) erosion of our international competitive advantage in equipment and machinery; (4) creation of future excess capacity to bedevil a post-Vietnam economy.

Against these, the economist balances the costs of action that might be taken to cut capital spending: (1) less rapid increase in manufacturing capacity for a Vietnam-charged economy;[5] (2) some reduction in employment opportunities; (3) interrupted modernization and expansion programs; (4) such intangible costs as possible loss of business confidence in the government's long-term commitment to a high-investment policy.

With this call-to-action balance in hand, the economist proceeds to factor out the comparative impacts of, say, tighter money, a surtax on corporate profits, and temporary suspension of the 7-percent tax credit for new investment.

His analysis will be designed to identify the policy step or steps that will most effectively, at minimum cost, cool off the immediate investment boom and transfer some of its force to a future period of economic ease. His job as an economist is not done until he has also measured and appraised the side effects, for example, on housing construction, on over-all consumer demand, on employment, on current and future rates of real growth, and on the balance of payments.

The estimates growing out of this analysis are bound to be imprecise and uncertain, but approximation and probability are the natural habitat of the economist. And his estimates will be far superior to intuition and guesswork. They will constantly grow in reliability as we sharpen our tools of economic analysis and enrich the flow of economic data. Needless to say, the policy appraisal does not stop with the economist. Equity, administrative, and political inputs still have to be fed into the decision mix. But the underlying cost-benefit balance will be struck by the economist in terms a decision maker can sink his teeth into.

The rising star of the political economist is also correlated with growing professional consensus. It is true that the shrill voices of minority groups, sharp debates over social goals, and differences in choice of weapons may obscure this now and then. For example, at the Twentieth Anniversary Symposium on the Employment Act of 1946, Leon Keyserling first expressed the hope that the previous evening's amicable dinner for program participants (including all six chairmen of the Council of Economic Advisers since its inception) would not "turn out to have been

the Last Supper," and then proceeded to liken the 1962–
1965 tax cuts to "$20 billion a year thrown into the
streets . . ." [6]

Yet, comparing economists of today with those of
twenty-five years ago, I am sure it is fair to say that there
is more of both the Keynesian and the conservative in us all.

It is often said that the study of economics makes people
conservative.[7] In the microeconomic sense, it undoubtedly
does. It is hard to study the modern economics of relative
prices, resource allocation, and distribution without developing a healthy respect for the market mechanism on
three major scores: first, for what Robert Dorfman calls its
"cybernetics," for the incredible capacity of the price system to receive and generate information and respond to
it;[8] second, for its technical efficiency and hard-headedness
as a guide to resources and a goad to effort and risk-taking;
and third, for its contribution to political democracy by
keeping economic decisions free and decentralized.

But I do not carry respect to the point of reverence. A
professional resolve to maintain our basic reliance on the
market process does not require us to admire or to tolerate
the resulting income distribution, or the existing division
of resources between the public and private sectors, or the
forces of monopoly and consumer deceit that tend to
thwart the market process. There are substantial differences
among economists on how far the government should go
in protecting consumers or setting guideposts for wages and
prices. But there is little difference — at least among the
vast majority of economists — in supporting strong measures to protect the free play of market forces against

monopoly and price-fixing, and in strongly opposing direct
wage and price controls as inefficient and inequitable substitutes for market forces, to be considered only as a last
resort in a war economy.

The study of macroeconomics, in turn, moves us in the
other direction. The basic structure of the Keynesian
theory of income and employment — and even the basic
strategies of Hansenian policy for stable full employment
— are now the village common of the economics community. When Milton Friedman, the chief guardian of
the *laissez-faire* tradition in American economics, said not
long ago, "We are all Keynesians now," [9] the profession
said "Amen."

True, we still differ over the tactics and timing of fiscal
and monetary moves for stabilization. We do not, for example, agree on precisely when we should tighten the
monetary and fiscal tourniquets in an overheating economy
or loosen them in a slack one. But we do agree that the
economy cannot regulate itself. We now take for granted
that the government must step in to provide the essential
stability at high levels of employment and growth that the
market mechanism, left alone, cannot deliver.

In other respects, too, conceptual advances and quantitative research in economics are replacing emotion with
reason. Advances in the theory and measurement of ex-
ternalities — of social benefits and costs — are leading to
greater agreement on the principles that should govern
where and how deeply government should enter into the
support of various functions. The relative dimensions of
private and social benefits of education, of scientific re-

search, of programs to control air and water pollution are better understood than ever before. There is still plenty of room for controversy on the degree and form of government action, but consensus on governing principles is growing.

An interesting sidelight is that even though the gap between economists and the public on Keynesian policy has been narrowing, the gap on the economics of the marketplace is still huge. A Gallup Poll early in 1966 found 45 percent of the American public saying "yes" to this question: Would a wage-price freeze as long as Vietnam lasts be a "good idea"? [10] Perhaps 90 percent of the economics profession would have thought it a bad idea. Why does this divergence not lead to friction and rejection as the earlier divergence on Keynesian policy did? Mainly, I believe, because there is a contradiction between the layman's pocketbook reaction and his ideology. And the most vocal groups who presume to speak for him regularly sound the trumpets for freedom from government interference. So, on proposals for wage and price controls, the *real* divergence between the economist and the public is greater than the *apparent* divergence. The economist finds himself, for a change, in the position of angel's advocate.

EXTERNAL FORCES

Perhaps the most potent force in the economist's rise to influence is the growing conviction of Presidents that effective economic policy is essential to their success as modern statesmen and as political leaders.

As a statesman, a President has a vital, not to say vested,

interest, on behalf of the nation, in prosperity and rapid growth. They put at his disposal, as nothing else can, the resources needed to achieve great societies at home and grand designs abroad. They enable him to meet their economic costs out of the real output and fiscal dividends generated by dynamic growth — and thus to press ahead with minimum social tension and economic dislocation.

Successful economic policies serve a President's international aims in three important ways:

(1) Materially, they provide the wherewithal for foreign aid and defense efforts and for financing Vietnam on a both-guns-and-butter basis.

(2) Ideologically, a vigorous American economy is a showcase of modern capitalism for all the world to see.

(3) Strategically, an expanding economy and a shrinking external payments deficit strengthen the President's hand in international politics.[11] The doubling of our growth rate in the past five years — moving it from the bottom to the top of the ladder among advanced nations — has strengthened not only the dollar but our strategic position in dealing with our free-world partners. What a change from 1961 when President Kennedy "ordered" me not to return from an international economic meeting in Paris until I had discovered the secret of European growth! What satisfaction he would have found in the "reverse lend-lease" of ideas which now finds European nations studying and borrowing some of the techniques of what President Johnson has called "the American economic miracle."

On the domestic front, policies that enable an economy

to grow and prosper give substance to Presidential pledges to "get the country moving again" or to move toward a great and good society. That society takes root far more readily in the garden of growth than in the desert of stagnation. When the cost of fulfilling a people's aspirations can be met out of a growing horn of plenty — instead of robbing Peter to pay Paul — ideological roadblocks melt away, and consensus replaces conflict.

As a political leader, President Johnson has found in modern economic policy an instrument that serves him well in giving form and substance to the stuff of which his dreams for America are made, in molding and holding a democratic consensus, and in giving that consensus a capital "D" in national elections. That the chill of recession may have tipped the Presidential election in 1960, and that the bloom of prosperity boosted the margin of victory in 1964, is widely acknowledged, especially by the defeated candidates.

At the 1966 Symposium on the Employment Act, there was much talk of the gradual evolution of economic policy under the terms of that act. But evolution became revolution the moment we had Presidents — and now we have had two — with the Keynesian perception to welcome their responsibilities under the act and to use its mandate and the weapons of political economy to generate both prosperity and the Presidential power that goes with it.

One uses the word "power" with some hesitation, for the growth of Federal or Presidential power is often identified with the decline of someone else's power and freedom. Economists might call this a "wages-fund theory of power"

— a plus here means a minus there. But a moment's reflection will show that this is simply not so.

Recent growth in Federal power in the economic realm has occurred side-by-side with growth of the effective freedom and strength of business and the individual. In spite of a guidepost here and a guideline there, a climate of vigorous growth has widened the range of choice of private enterprise and made it more vibrant, competitive, and open to the entry of new ideas, new products, and new businesses. And decentralized decision making and freedom of choice are left untouched by the impersonal fiscal and monetary tools that government uses to carry out its responsibility for a high-level economy under the Employment Act.

As to the individual, abundance enlarges his options, his meaningful freedom to choose among goods and services, among jobs, and between work and leisure. Prosperity extends economic freedom more deeply, creating jobs and enabling a President to battle the tyranny of poverty for some without wrenching resources away from others. In the battle against discrimination, prosperity adds economic rights to civil rights. Thus economic liberty can grow — indeed, is growing — simultaneously with governmental power.

Given the uses of political economy as a source of effective Presidential power; given the compatibility, in this context, of power with freedom; and given the statutory responsibility for maintaining prosperity in an economy that, by its nature, cannot be self-regulating, one finds it hard to imagine a future President spurning professional economic advice and playing a passive economic role. The words and deeds of today's leading Republican candidates and Democratic heirs-apparent would seem to lend substance to this conclusion. In political economics, the day of the Neanderthal Man — indeed, the day of the pre-Keynesian Man — is past.

THE ECONOMIST AS PRESIDENTIAL ADVISER

For the reasons I have reviewed, then, I believe that the political economist is now a fixture in the high councils of government. Not that his position, even apart from personalities, will ever be entirely secure or settled. The skeptic may well ask:

• Won't Say's Law of Economic Advice — successful advice creates its own demand — work in reverse when expansion turns into inflation, when forecasts go sour, when good economics clashes with good politics?

• Won't Presidential enthusiasm wane when the policy coin is turned over, and the motto reads not "fiscal dividends" but "fiscal drag," not "tax cuts" but "tax increases"?

• Won't faith in economists ebb because people now expect more of them than they can deliver?

Admittedly, there is some quicksand here — but bedrock is only a few inches down. Bedrock, as we have seen, consists of the increasing power and reliability of the tools that economists bring to their trade; a growing consensus on the analytical core of economics; lessons of performance well done that will not easily be undone; the fact that active economic policy, whatever its limitations, is indispensable to the highest purposes of the Presidency.

I doubt that a new chairman of the Council of Economic Advisers will ever again be asked, as I was late in 1960: "Will you handle this from Minnesota, or will you have to go to Washington?" And never again will a member of the Council call his position, as one did in the 1950's, the "highest paid fellowship in the profession." The detached, Olympian, take-it-or-leave-it approach to Presidential economic advice — the dream of the logical positivist — simply does not accord with the demands of relevance and realism and the requirements of the Employment Act.

ADVISORY FUNCTIONS

What *are* the Presidential adviser's responsibilities to the President, to the public, to the profession, and to himself? I do not, by the way, necessarily identify "economic adviser" with "Council of Economic Advisers." The President receives economic advice from many other sources both inside and outside of the government — I don't know why, but the Treasury readily comes to mind — and even from sources that are "independent in, but not of, the Government." Yet, the forces of both law and practice make it increasingly natural that the major focus of Presidential economic advice should be in the Council. So even when I use the term "economic advisers" generically, the reader will usually be right if he subconsciously adds the prefix, "Council of."

The major functions of the economic adviser, as I have

seen and known them, are to analyze, interpret, and forecast; to give policy advice; to educate; and to adapt and
translate.[12]

Economic analysis, interpretation, and forecasting. The
unique function of the Council of Economic Advisers is to
put at the President's disposal the best facts, appraisals, and
forecasts that economic science, statistics, and surveys can
produce. Under the terms of the Employment Act, the
Council assesses for the President both "current and foreseeable economic trends" and the levels of economic activity needed to carry out the policy of the act.[13] Beyond
this, the advisers supply him — at times, he must think,
bombard him — with a steady stream of searching memoranda on the whole spectrum of economic issues. Important
economic developments and events are analyzed and interpreted, not merely in the sense of how and why they
occurred, but what they signify, and what their future con-
sequences are likely to be. In addition, President Johnson
has assured himself of a continuous flow of current economic intelligence by setting up a system of thrice-weekly
"economic news notes" — brief reports of economic news,
both good and bad, with interpretive comments by CEA
members. In recent years, a substantial part of the economic
analysis undertaken within the Administration has been
made available to the Congress and the public through
the Council's *Annual Report*, testimony, statements, and
speeches.

Policy advice. On a foundation of such analysis and fact,
and in the normative environment of Employment Act
mandates and basic Presidential philosophy, the economic

adviser weighs the contributions of various courses of action to the competing objectives of economic policy. Not ignoring administrative and political feasibility, he presses the case for some measures and against others. Often he serves up alternatives and points up conflicting economic and political hazards. But when the President asks what, all things considered, is his advice, he must be prepared to answer. As Gardner Ackley recently put it: "If his economic adviser refrains from advice on the gut questions of policy, the President should and will get another one." [14] Happily for the economic adviser, politics and economics are often in harmony rather than conflict. For him, happiness is a political need that can be filled by an economic good.

Education. Experience of recent years has demonstrated that education — of the President, by the President, and for the President — is an inescapable part of an economic adviser's function. The explanatory and analytical models of the economist must be implanted — at least intuitively — in the minds of Presidents, congressmen, and public leaders if economic advice is to be accepted and translated into action. I deal with this important function at some length below.

Adaptation and translation. In listing this as a separate function, I run the risk of overlap with the analysis and education functions. Nonetheless it is such a vital activity of the adviser — and yet one so often dimly perceived by observers — that it merits separate listing. To take the highly refined and purified concepts of economics and to convert them into workable and digestible form for service as policy guides and focal points for consensus — that is, to move economics from a point several abstractions away from the real world right to ground zero — involves a constant process of adaptation, translation, and innovation. The operational concepts of the "production gap," "full-employment surplus," the "fiscal drag," and "fiscal dividends" illustrate this process.[15] The terms in which problems are put, even their simple semantics, have an important bearing on the fixing of political objectives and the formation of policy. As Irving Babbitt said, "All great revolutions are preceded by a revolution in the dictionary." [16]

ISSUES IN ADVISORY RESPONSIBILITY

The foregoing functions inevitably raise some issues of responsible behavior for the economic adviser. They involve him in value choices, in advocacy of Presidential programs, and in balancing what is ideal against what is practicable. And they push him to the outer limits of his data and analysis, and sometimes beyond. Let me offer a few personal observations on how one resolves some of these issues. If, perchance, there is a grain or two of eternal truth in these observations, so much the better.

Value choices. Implicit in a great deal of what I have already said is that value judgments are an inescapable, obligatory, and desirable part of the life of an economic adviser.

Value judgments are *inescapable*, because, as Arthur Smithies pointed out some years ago, "Concern with policy . . . must be based on ethical or political presuppositions derived from the non-economic world." [17] Merely selecting objectives for economic policy, as one must, involves us in normative choices. "Full employment," "high growth," and "price stability" may have a hard economic ring, but they are only proxies, if you will, for such social goals as personal fulfillment, a rising quality of life, and equity between fixed and variable income recipients. As we said in the 1962 *Annual Report*: "The ultimate goals of the Nation are human goals, and . . . economics is merely instrumental to the making of a better life for all Americans. Involuntary unemployment is a sign of economic waste, but the fundamental evil of unemployment is that it is an affront to human dignity." [18]

Value judgments are *obligatory* under the Employment Act, which requires the setting of target levels of employment, production, and purchasing power. Where? At unemployment rates of 5 percent, or 4, or 3? At average factory operating rates of 90, or 92, or 94 percent of capacity? At annual growth rates of 3, or 4, or 5 percent? In answering those questions, we are not making coldly scientific judgments, but value choices between higher prices and more jobs, between current consumption and investment in the future, and so on.

Value judgments are *desirable*, for to say anything of importance in the policy process requires such judgments. For example, meeting the added costs of Vietnam by higher taxes rather than Great Society cutbacks is not just an economic but a social choice. The choice of higher taxes gives content to President Johnson's eloquent pledge to "call for the contribution of those who live in the fullness of our blessing, rather than try to strip it from the hands

of those that are most in need." [19] Technical advice divorced
from such value preferences will have a hollow ring to
those in authority.

The intimate connection between values and analysis,
between technical and social goals, was well illustrated in
the original economic thinking that underlay the poverty
program. As early as May 1963, Kenneth O'Donnell told
me: "Stop worrying about the tax cut. It will pass — and
pass big. Worry about something else." We did. We
turned to the question of those whom the tax cut would
leave behind. Our analysis showed that the tax cut would
create two to three million additional jobs and thus open
many new exits from poverty. But those caught in the web
of illiteracy, lack of skills, poor health, and squalor would
not be able to make use of these exits.

A full-fledged response to the Employment Act's in-
sistence on "useful employment opportunities . . . for
those able, willing, and seeking to work" had to go beyond
tax cuts and fiscal policy to entirely new measures focused
sharply and specifically on removal of the roadblocks of
poverty. By mid-1963, I had sent President Kennedy our
economic and statistical analysis of the groups beyond the
reach of the tax cut and had offered some groping thoughts
on "an attack on poverty." Obviously, we were deep in the
realm of social goals and values. But much of the problem,
and much of the solution, was economic in nature. I do not
feel that I strayed beyond my preserve as economic adviser.

The danger, then, does not lie in admitting, or even wel-
coming, values to the economic advisory process. Danger
would exist were value choices permitted to warp the

economist's advice and slant his facts and analysis. If the adviser were to cloak his value preferences in the guise of scientific findings, he would of course be unfit to serve.

Advocacy. Much has been written about the hazards of open advocacy — of explanation and defense of Presidential policy — by economic advisers. The fear is that they may lose their professional objectivity and integrity in the process. But as the Kennedy CEA said in its first appearance before the Joint Economic Committee of Congress in March 1961 (in which it set new precedents both by appearing in open, rather than executive, session and by submitting and releasing a prepared statement): "The Council has a responsibility to explain to the Congress and to the public the general economic strategy of the President's program, especially as it relates to the objectives of the Employment Act." [20]

Such explanation, it seems to me, is essential to the understanding, acceptance, and adoption of sound economic policy. Some have said, "Explanation, yes; defense, no." But to draw a line between the two is next to impossible. And within reasonable bounds, it is unnecessary. Again, as we stated in 1961: "The Council is, and necessarily must be, in harmony with the general aims and direction of the President and his Administration. A member of the Council who felt otherwise would resign." And we added: "This general harmony is, of course, consistent with divergences of views on specific issues." [21]

Advocacy poses no insoluble problems of integrity and few of objectivity (though silence may occasionally be golden) under circumstances that surely characterize the years since 1961: first, a general harmony of objectives between President and Council; second, a Presidential readiness to heed (if not always to follow) the Council's analysis and advice; and third, an Administration economic policy bearing the Council's imprint in both content and direction.

Of course, the adviser will not always get his way — nor should he. Some policy measures may be ruled out at a given time — perhaps by a conflicting Presidential commitment, by an insurmountable congressional obstacle, or by an unready public opinion wedded to shibboleths not yet unlearned. In that case, the ideal solution may have to yield to "second best." To explain and defend a *good* policy measure under circumstances where the *best* is beyond the political pale need not offend the conscience of the economist.

At times, the view of the economic advisers *does* diverge from that of the President. It did in 1962 when the Council was privately urging a large tax cut that President Kennedy was not yet ready to endorse. Under such circumstances, selective silence, publicly, is the adviser's best defense of integrity and credibility. "Where politics has necessarily overruled economics," Theodore Sorensen has observed, ". . . the economic adviser should not use his skills and reputation to justify the unjustifiable if he is to retain his effectiveness with his professional colleagues, the Congress, the public, and ultimately the President." [22] In this context, advisers need to keep in mind the warning voiced by Allan Sproul: "The silence which should occasionally be golden may succumb more and more to the lure of the lectern as the warmth of a place near the throne inflames the blood." [23]

Open advocacy carries with it certain other discomforts. When the adviser takes to the economic stump, he has to make a more conscious effort to stay within the bounds of his professional competence. And the public makes no fine distinctions — in advocacy, the political economist is seen as more "political" than "economist."

He should also be prepared to serve as a lightning rod for the angry charges generated by offended vested interests and prejudices — a consequence that is as convenient for Presidents as it is uncomfortable for advisers. The wage-price guideposts have been a prolific source of such charges against the Council, and the AFL-CIO carried them to a new peak of intensity in 1966. Accusations of fiscal irresponsibility reached their peak early in 1963, just after President Kennedy proposed a massive tax cut in the face of a rising deficit, rising expenditures, and a rising economy. Hugh Sidey's book, *John F. Kennedy, President*, reminds me that the President interrupted our conversation one day during that period and said, "Walter, I want to make it perfectly clear that I resent these attacks on you." [24]

Maintaining objectivity and perspective. Difficult as it may be for the citizen to discern, there is a deep professional commitment that serves as a safeguard against loss of professional objectivity. The adviser knows he has to answer not only to himself but to his profession as well. This commitment is strengthened by our American practice — one might almost say our "system" — of moving advisers back and forth between academic and government life. The close tie with his professional base and the prospect of re-

turning to it after a period of service in government prevent
the subtle accretion of hostages to a political environment
— hostages, not to special interest groups, but to Presidential preferences — which might eventually impair objectivity and bias judgment. This "in-and-out" character-
istic of American economic advising substitutes, in a sense,
for the British career-service tradition as insurance of
objectivity.

In addition to objectivity, modesty becomes advisers.
They need to recognize the limitations of their tools, the
role of luck, the role of the private sector, and the restrictions imposed by various "realities":

• Staying within the technical limits of his analysis and
information is essential to confidence in the adviser. This
means that he sometimes has to say "I don't know" even
when an educated guess might seem a manlier way out. At
other times, it means identifying (both to himself and to
others) the gaps in his data and analysis. But it does *not*
mean that he has to forswear judgments and advice until
all the facts and analyses are in. If it did, he would stand
mute a good part of the time. In the course of a hearing
before the Joint Economic Committee in 1959, I observed
that "policy itself must be made humbly and hesitantly in
the light of imperfect knowledge . . . policy decisions
cannot wait until knowledge is perfected." Senator Douglas
quickly replied in the words of Justice Oliver Wendell
Holmes: "Every year, if not every day, we have to wager
our salvation upon some prophecy based on imperfect
knowledge." [25]

• Aptness in government economic policy is based not

only on good facts, good analysis, and good timing — it also requires good judgment, good nerves, and above all, good luck. For example, though the tax cut chiefly reflects the first five items in the list, it was the Council's good luck — just when the skeptical, not to say hostile, spotlight was full upon it — to have the 1964 tax cut come when the economy was still moving forward. If the impact of the tax cut had instead offset an incipient downturn, holding the economy up but not moving it spectacularly ahead, we would have lost the force of the *post hoc, ergo propter hoc* reasoning that has undoubtedly played an important role in gaining popular acceptance for positive fiscal policy.

• Economic advisers are sometimes accused of acting as though they alone were carrying and balancing economic expansion on their shoulders. This accusation goes too far. But the view from the third floor of the Executive Office Building does not always have the private economy in sharp focus. The political economist is well advised to recognize that a key factor, not only in the length and strength but particularly in the balance of the great expansion of the 1960's, has been the impact of effective private policies — better inventory and cost control, less speculation, better matching of plant capacity to markets, and more restrained wage-price policies than we have had in any previous expansion in our history.

• The economist on the policy firing line clearly has fewer options than the academic economist because he has to operate within the limits not only of his scientific knowledge but of political reality, public understanding, and institutional rigidities (like fixed exchange rates, a lengthy

legislative process, and so forth). Unlike his academic col-
league who can abstract from reality, deal with ultimates,
and envision quantum jumps in our progress toward the
ideal economic state, the economic practitioner has to
operate deep in the heart of realism, has to deal with movement *toward* rather than *to* the ideal, and has to be at all
times multidimensional in his objectives. The lump-sum tax
— economically, the best of all taxes — will never replace
the lump of taxes we now live with. And the principle that
a change is good if the gainers could more than compensate
the losers — the central policy precept of formal welfare
economics — is a sterile guide when, in practice, the compensation can never be made. All this exaggerates my point,
particularly since many academic economists are themselves
at the forefront in providing realistic analysis and policy
proposals. But it does illustrate the gulf that often separates
economic science, with its limitations, from economic practice, with its. Although the gulf will never be entirely
bridged, an important part of the adviser's job is to push
out the boundaries of the possible in public policy, especially those that are set by lack of economic understanding.

ECONOMIC EDUCATION OF, BY, AND
FOR PRESIDENTS

President Kennedy, early in January 1961, urged me "to
use the White House as a pulpit for public education in
economics, especially on the desirable effects of a Federal
deficit in a recession" (quickly adding, "but always make
clear that the recession started *last* year"). He plainly

recognized — even if his own economic thinking was still in its formative stage — that the major barrier to getting the country's economy moving again lay in the economic ignorance and stereotypes that prevailed in the land. The copybook maxims of private finance misapplied to Federal finance threatened to strangle expansionary policy.

As Norton Long has put it: "Both the limits of popular knowledge and the relation of popularly accepted values to permissible practice are basic conditions defining the politically feasible . . . Natural rights, individualism, and the teachings of classical economics are profoundly hostile to attempts to render the economy politically responsible." [26]

In 1961, with over five million unemployed and a production gap of nearly $50 billion, the problem of the economic adviser was not what to say, but how to get people to listen. Even the President could not adopt modern economic advice, however golden, as long as the Congress and the public "knew" that it was only fool's gold. The power of Keynesian ideas could not be harnessed to the nation's lagging economy without putting them in forms and terms that could be understood in the sense of fitting the vocabulary and the values of the public. At the same time, men's minds had to be conditioned to accept new thinking, new symbols, and new and broader concepts of the public interest.

Small wonder that the President and his advisers had to devote time not only to developing what was economically workable but to extending the boundaries of what was politically marketable.

In this process, we were painfully aware of the force of Jefferson's observation that a person "is less remote from the truth who believes nothing, than he who believes what is wrong." How could the forces of modern economics be mobilized in the public interest in the face of the misplaced but deeply ingrained fears of government deficits, debts, and spending? Indeed, these fears or bogies had been strengthened rather than weakened by obeisance in high places in the previous Administration. And Gunnar Myrdal bitingly reminded us that America's economists were in part to blame, having devoted far too little time to the task of public education in economics.

But the difficulty went beyond the economic state of the popular mind. The patterns of professional thought and practice that prevailed in previous economic policy making had not given full scope to the concepts and techniques of modern economics:

• Policy thinking had been centered more on minimizing the fluctuations of the business cycle than on realizing the economy's great and growing potential. As Arthur Burns said in 1960: "the American people have of late been more conscious of the business cycle, more sensitive to every wrinkle of economic curves, more alert to the possible need for contracyclical action on the part of government, than ever before in our history." [27]

• There was no standard apparatus for setting the quantitative employment and output targets called for by the provisions of the Employment Act, provisions that for some years had been largely ignored.

• Even after inflationary forces had ebbed, the continued fear of inflation kept policy thinking in too restrictive a mold in the late 1950's.

To redirect the focus, fill the vacuum, and instill confidence in the tools of the economist was an indispensable prelude to the modernization of economic policy. In the next chapter, I will deal with our early efforts to recast the standards of economic performance in more ambitious terms, in terms more suitable to the tremendous capabilities of the U.S. economy.

EDUCATION OF PRESIDENTS

Coupled with the obstacles that faced the economic advisers of the sixties was the unprecedented opportunity of working with two Presidents who for the first time opened the White House gates wide to the "new economics." Their minds were remarkably receptive to new economic ideas and policies, remarkably free of the preconceived doctrines that one might naturally associate with their backgrounds. They were deeply committed to more rapid growth as an instrument of the common good and eager to put the power of modern economics to work to help them achieve the nation's goals. And they had insatiable appetites for memoranda written by their economic advisers — over 300 economic memoranda went to President Kennedy in the thousand days of his Presidency, and the volume has risen under President Johnson.

But "unprecedented opportunity" should not be read to mean "easy pickings," as a leaf or two from the chronicle of President Kennedy's development as an economist will quickly reveal. Much has already been told. From it one might gain an impression of more or less steady progression to economic sophistication and bold expansionary policy. But seen from close by, the course of true economics was not always smooth and straight.

As I reflect on the early months of the Kennedy Administration, I must agree with those who feel that, judged only in terms of policies actually proposed and adopted, modern economics established a firm beachhead on the New Frontier, but not much more, in 1961. And one should probably heed the judgment of authorities like Seymour Harris that Kennedy "at first seemed allergic to modern economics." [28] One should not infer, however, that his allergy was inbred. Much of it was simply a political sensitivity to the sting of Republican charges of fiscal irresponsibility and a consciousness that tax cuts did not fit his call for sacrifice. Several incidents in 1961 seem to confirm that economic reason and political reality pulled Kennedy in opposite directions.

As economists, we were shocked when we were told in one of our first White House meetings that the antirecession battle would have to be fought within the bounds of a balanced budget. But relief followed shock when, with our help, the commitment was watered down to read in the State of the Union Message: "Within that framework [that is, of the Eisenhower spending and revenue estimates], barring the development of urgent national defense needs or a worsening of the economy, it is my current intention to advocate a program of expenditures which, including revenues from a stimulation of the economy, will not of and by themselves unbalance the earlier Budget." [29] We counted seven escape hatches.

Subsequently, in his February 2 message "proposing a program to restore momentum to the American economy," Kennedy said on one hand that "the Federal budget can and should be made an instrument of prosperity and stability, not a deterrent to recovery"; on the other, he pledged budget balance over the economic cycle. He also introduced the concept of the production gap (the gap between actual and potential output), noting that "even when the recession ends and economic activity begins to expand again, the problem of unused potential will remain." [30] However, to our disappointment, he did not follow up with a bold second-stage recovery program.

Later, when he reviewed a draft of the Council's March 6 testimony before the Joint Economic Committee, he showed great Keynesian promise by suggesting that one of the paragraphs in our testimony be recast to read, in part: "The success of fiscal and budget policies cannot be measured only by whether the budget is in the black or in the red. The true test is whether the economy is in balance . . . If at the end of this year the unemployment ratio is still near seven percent, our fiscal policies would have to be viewed with great concern, even if there is little or no deficit in the budget." [31] Yet the words "even if" instead of "especially if" suggested that his conversion still had some distance to go.

But as recovery waxed during 1961, his interest in economic matters temporarily waned. Sorensen, seeing the three Council members (Kermit Gordon, James Tobin, and the author) in somewhat solemn conclave at the White House Staff Mess one day, called out, "There they are, contemplating the dangers of an upturn!"

A low point was reached in the summer of 1961 when Kennedy, flying in the face of modern economics, tentatively decided on a tax increase of $3 billion to finance the Berlin defense buildup in spite of the still-yawning gap between the economy's actual and potential performance. The Council, though ably represented by Sorensen in meetings of the National Security Council (which we did not attend), fought a lonely and losing battle against this decision until a narrow corridor of power, the small corridor leading into the oval office of the President, was opened by O'Donnell. His sympathetic intercession provided access to the President on this issue and enabled us to set forces in motion that brought a reversal of his tentative decision. Another strategically placed ally, Paul Samuelson, helped the cause with a timely visit to Hyannis Port on the weekend just before the final decision.

Kennedy linked his Berlin no-tax decision with a firm pledge of a balanced budget for the fiscal year 1963. With the recovery proceeding briskly in mid-1961, this looked like a reasonable target, even with rising expenditures. But eventually the President found that he had to "paper over" a deficit in order to move ahead on his expenditure programs and get what we hoped would be a sufficiently stimulative budget. One day in October he recalled with some admiration Roosevelt's and Eisenhower's abilities to talk balanced budgets even in the face of repeated deficits. Increasingly he was trying to find ways of reconciling sensible economic policy with popular values that, however mistaken, could not be transformed overnight.

In 1962 Kennedy responded much more positively to the challenge of Keynesian economics and to the promise of bold policies for expansion. The progression was unmistakable, even if not unbroken.

By June of 1962, after the recovery faltered, Kennedy issued his own declaration of economic independence in the justly famous Yale speech on economic mythology. As his economic advisers, we were confident that this speech marked a new era in American economic policy. His decision two months later to call for a massive tax cut early in 1963 confirmed this.

Yet there was many a thorn among the roses in the summer of 1962. Logic called for immediate fiscal action to overcome persistent economic slack and, more urgently, to deal with the unexpected slowdown of recovery in mid-1962. But political barriers did not succumb readily to the force of economic logic. Kennedy was persuaded that he could not get swift action from a Congress still bound in large part by the very mythology he had attacked at Yale. So our hopes for a "quickie tax cut" — a temporary cut in 1962 to serve as the first installment of the basic tax reduction required to remove fiscal drag — had to give way to his commitment to act in 1963. That commitment, of course, did represent a fundamental turn in policy.

But lapses do occur. Even Presidents have self-doubts. One of my most unsettling days as economic adviser was Friday, December 14, 1962. My notes for that day tell me:

"As of the moment, the President is shaken on the question of the tax cut . . . I have never seen the President so anguished and uncertain about the correctness of his course on a domestic matter in the two years that I have served with him." I noted that his reaction was a response to three events.

First, he had received a phone call from Senator Robert S. Kerr saying that the economic outlook for 1963, even without the tax cut, was getting better and better, so why cut taxes in an upswing?

Second, the long shadow of our Ambassador to India, John Kenneth Galbraith, had fallen across the White House with a renewed call for expenditure increases rather than tax cuts in the face of vast unmet needs for public services.

Third, at a Cabinet meeting the previous Monday, the President had, at my urging, asked his Cabinet members for reactions to the projected $10 billion tax cut. The results were a small disaster. Departmental interests in bigger expenditure programs won out over the general interest in a tax cut. Had the Cabinet been a decision-making body, the tax cut might have sunk on that reef even though not far beyond were the deeper and calmer economic waters of a great prosperity in which great budgets would be easier to finance.

I restated to the President, as strongly as I could, the conviction of his economic advisers that the economy had plenty of room for the stimulus of the tax cut and that the resulting prosperity would generate huge revenues to finance the programs envisaged by Cabinet members and ambassadors. Although he seemed somewhat reassured, his doubts on that Friday were still deep.

Fortunately the mood did not last long. After his superbly successful tax speech to the Economic Club of New York the next day, his enthusiasm for the tax cut returned. He phoned to say, "I gave them straight Keynes and Heller, and they loved it." From that point on, Kennedy moved steadily ahead on the tax-cut course and the educational job needed to put it across.

In that educational process he still felt uncertain that one could persuade Congress to enact a big tax cut simply on the basis that a fiscal overburden was retarding the advance of the economy. As a consequence he rattled the recession skeleton in 1963. This may have quickened the pulses of a few congressmen, but it also muddied the educational waters. For it temporarily put the tax cut back into a short-run anticyclical context rather than keeping its focus where it belonged, namely, on the removal of fiscal roadblocks to longer-run expansion.

Nevertheless, President Kennedy's occasional doubts and concessions to prevailing economic sentiment stand out only as detours on his road to modernism. What was pleasing to his economic advisers, and fortunate for the country, was his responsiveness to *analysis*, the force of economic logic and fact; to *analogy*, the demonstrated success of Keynesian policies abroad; and to *anomaly*, the continued sacrifice of human and material resources on the altar of false concepts of "sound finance."

President Johnson's background, like that of his predecessor, conditioned him to fiscal caution, if not conservatism.

But he also shared with Kennedy a growing impatience with the performance of the economy and a willingness to explore the potential of new economic ideas. There is this difference: actual *performance*, the hard evidence of results flowing from policy action, looms larger in President Johnson's economic thinking. And by the time he became President, some of the results *were* flowing from the 1962 fiscal actions and related stimulants.

Fortunately, after President Johnson drove the tax cut through to enactment early in 1964, the economy responded almost exactly in accord with the economic analysis and projections on which it was founded. It made good on both its economic and its budgetary promises. The slow yeast of change that had been working to raise public understanding of new economic ideas now gave way, under the impact of the tax cut, to rapid changes in public thinking and acceptance of active fiscal policy. And in the process, President Johnson (who had once described his economics to me as "old fashioned") turned quickly, smoothly, and effectively to the uses of modern economics.

EDUCATION BY PRESIDENTS

John F. Kennedy and Lyndon B. Johnson stand out, then, as the first modern economists in the American Presidency. Their Administrations were largely free of the old mythology and wrong-headed economics which had viewed government deficits as synonymous with inflation; government spending increases as a likely source of depressions that would "curl your hair"; and government debts as an immoral burden on our grandchildren. These avowed Presidential and Cabinet views of less than ten years ago serve as vivid reminders of how far we have advanced through the leadership of two Presidents who typically talked economic sense to the American people and matched good sense with good policy.

President Kennedy's landmark speech at Yale stands as the most literate and sophisticated dissertation on economics ever delivered by a President (and he wrote much of it himself). In that speech, in his two annual Economic Messages, in two nationwide television talks on the tax cut, in press conferences, in White House statements, and in speeches, he put Presidential economic discourse on a wholly new plane.

In economic policy, he molded the diversity among his advisers (in the CEA, Treasury, and the Budget Bureau in particular, but also in Labor, Commerce, and other departments) into a harmonious consensus. He was thereby able to put the full weight of his Administration behind bold and modern economic measures like the tax cut.

His policy declarations, in economics as in other fields, were ringing documents, full of drama, challenge, and call-to-arms.

The education-and-consensus process has undergone some change in President Johnson's hands. He too has achieved remarkable internal consensus on policy, but has gone beyond this to externalize it. When public discussion of major issues reaches an appropriate point, the White House seeks agreement, or at least understanding, on program proposals among leaders of Congress and the pertinent private groups on whom legislative and popular support heavily depends.

Presidential policy pronouncements tend to be in a low key, muting points of controversy and difference, and treating new policy measures as natural, almost self-evident, moves for a prosperous, mature, and modern nation to make. Conflict is minimized. Support is maximized. And the results are counted on not only to benefit but to educate the country. As I perceive it, then, this method combines Presidential persuasion and education of hundreds of the country's "movers and shakers" *in person* in small White House meetings and large with public persuasion of millions of citizens by *performance* under the resulting policies and legislation.

The London *Economist* views this process with some awe, "not so much as a new ideology as 'the end of ideology' . . . an end of a vast amount of ritualistic response. This perhaps is the great Johnson achievement — much of it the age-old political achievement of unleashing actions from the deadweight of cripplingly loaded words." [Government aims and responsibility are presented] "as common and necessary goals . . . for which he has a right to expect a consensus of opinion rather than partisan action bitterly fought." [32]

In the search for consensus on responsible use of fiscal and monetary powers to achieve growth and stability, both Presidents recognized that it was necessary to make concessions to popular economic ideology and precepts. Their responsibilities as national leaders did not permit them to wait until the economic intelligence gap had been closed. So they drew on what Norton Long calls "the great psychological assets of sailing under the familiar colors." [33] In that vein, Sorensen described the economics of Kennedy's New York speech a bit differently than the President had: "It sounded like Hoover, but it was actually Heller." [34]

How great is the danger that this approach will fail to develop the longer-run understanding of, and ideological support for, aggressive economic policies? Acceptance of the huge tax cut was gained in part by claiming (a) that it was the surest way to achieve a balanced budget in a balanced economy, (b) that the debt would still drop as a proportion of GNP, and (c) that rigid frugality would be practiced in the Federal budget. My academic instinct is to say that, even though these claims were valid, the homage thus paid to balanced budgets and the hostages thus given to the old deficit, debt, and spending phobias will rise to haunt us in later efforts.[35]

But the 1964 tax cut and its impact on the tenor of fiscal debate lead me to hope that my instinctive answer is wrong. Why?

First, because although the arguments for the tax cut were poured into old molds, its success cracked, perhaps even shattered, those molds of ideology and error.

Second, because the arguments themselves were, to a significant degree, new in content. Thus, a balanced budget was to be sought not every year, nor even over the cycle, but at full employment; not in the administrative, but in the national-income-accounts budget. The implicit standard for national debt reduction was shifted from an absolute to a relative basis — the national debt should decline as a proportion of GNP. As to deficits, a new distinction was drawn between "deficits of weakness" that arise out of backing into a recession and "deficits of strength" that arise out of measures to provide fiscal thrust to a lagging economy. And, in government spending, sin is now correctly identified not with spending more dollars per se, but with failure to deliver "a dollar's worth of value for a dollar spent." So the standards of fiscal soundness, even while "sailing under the familiar colors," have become more modern and rational.

One need only recall the wave of fear and ridicule touched off by the tax-cut idea in 1962 and 1963, in contrast with the calm acceptance of the excise tax cuts in 1965, to conclude that in this case expediency may have been the mother of principle. A skilled interplay of results and ideas can be one of the highest expressions of Presidential leadership.

Let me make clear that I am *not* defending acceptance without understanding, consent without comprehension. Nor do I believe that the demonstration that "it works" can, or should, be counted on to do the whole educational job. The results and their lessons must be articulated, preferably by Presidents, for "The dark is the breeding ground of the myth that the workings of the economy must be left to the play of autonomous forces." [36]

Yet nothing succeeds like success. The tax cut has opened minds and let new ideas in. It has led to a growing consensus — at a higher level of understanding — on the active use of government economic tools to manage prosperity. Even though politics will at times blunt the use of these tools, the level of economic debate, and hence the quality of economic policy decisions, has been permanently raised.

EDUCATION FOR PRESIDENTS

In part, the economic adviser's educational activity on behalf of the President is simply a case of doing on a small scale — though with greater detail, depth, and diligence — what the President does on a grand scale, namely, *communication*, making the government's economic policy and action intelligible to the citizen, a process essential to democracy; and *broadening consensus*, carrying the economic gospel not only to the uninformed but to the skeptic and the heathen.

But, in part, economic advisers are also expected to do things that the President, given the nature and demands of his office, is in a poor position to do.

Dialogue in depth. The explaining of economic concepts and the implanting of new ideas — especially when they conflict with established doctrine — involve a willing adviser not only in numerous speeches, radio and television appearances, and background meetings with the press, but also in countless meetings with representatives of labor, business, finance, consumers, agriculture, and the professions. The Employment Act wisely provides that the Council "may constitute such advisory committees . . . as it deems advisable." Presidents Kennedy and Johnson both encouraged the Council to establish such committees and use them actively as instruments of the two-way communication and understanding that must precede consensus.

More or less regular meetings with business and labor leaders and their chief economists have been an excellent vehicle for constructive and frank exchanges of views. These and other meetings enable the Council not only to explain its ideas but to take the pulse and test the temper of private economic opinion — and to forward its findings to the President.

As part of their concept of responsibility to the Congress and the public, the Kennedy and Johnson councils have made a practice of appearing in open sessions before congressional committees. Most of these appearances are before the Council's congressional counterpart under the Employment Act, the Joint Economic Committee. The work of that committee, though not part of my subject here, has been a vital factor in the broadening of congressional and popular understanding of modern economics. Council appearances before other committees have been limited, with very few exceptions, to situations calling for general economic information, analysis, and evaluation.

Testing new ideas: the wage-price guideposts. Professional advisers are in a position to test new concepts and broad policy approaches for the President — being careful not to close options by seeming to commit him to a particular course of action. President Kennedy, in particular, encouraged the Council to get out a bit ahead of him in the battle to gain acceptance of modern economics and its policy precepts. He would say to us, "I can't say that yet, but you can." In the television "Westerns," they would say we were "riding point." Both the pleasures and the dangers of that position are obvious.

In a sense the price-wage guideposts exemplify this role of the Council. It was in the Council's, not the President's, January 1962, *Annual Report* that the guideposts were stated for the first time.[37] And although Administration wage-price policy was soon shaped around them, they were pointedly called "the Council's guideposts" both within and without the Administration. They had the President's blessing, but not, at first, a tight embrace. Increasingly under President Kennedy and fully under President Johnson, they became Presidential guideposts.

They fit well under the heading of "Education" because they rely for much of their effectiveness on their informational content — their specification of responsible wage-price behavior. In essence they pit the power of public opinion and Presidential persuasion against the market power of strong unions and strong businesses. They try to bring to the bargaining tables and board rooms where wage and price decisions are made a sense of the public interest in noninflationary wage and price behavior. Indeed, they try to appeal also to labor and management's broad self-interest in avoiding a self-defeating price-wage spiral.

Their major thrust, then, has been through the process of informing labor, management, and the public of the explicit ways in which wage and price decisions should be geared to productivity advances if they are to be noninflationary. Under the guideposts, wage rate increases averaging no more than the average national increase in productivity — about 3.2 percent annually as of 1966 — are seen as noninflationary. To maintain over-all price stability, price reductions in industries with above-average produc-

tivity advances should roughly offset increases in those with
below-average advances.

One cannot say exactly how much of the moderation in
wages and prices in 1961–1965 should be attributed to the
guideposts. But one can say that their educational impact
has been impressive. They have significantly advanced the
rationality of the wage-price dialogue.

In *business*, the guideposts have contributed, first, to a
growing recognition that rising wages are not synonymous
with rising costs *per unit* of output. As long as the pay
for an hour's work does not rise faster than the products of
an hour's work, rising wages are consistent with stable or
falling unit-labor costs. Second, they are helping lay to
rest the old fallacy that "if productivity rises 3 percent and
wages rise 3 percent, labor is harvesting all the fruits of
productivity." Guidepost thinking makes it clear that a
3-percent rise in labor's total compensation, which is about
three fifths of private GNP, still leaves a 3-percent gain on
the remaining two fifths — enough to provide ample rewards to capital, as is vividly demonstrated by the doubling
of corporate profits after taxes in the five years between the
first quarters of 1961 and 1966.

In *labor*, the guideposts have helped bring home the idea
that wages are not simply purchasing power, but costs.
Average wage gains that stay within bounds of average
productivity gains will endure, while "gains achieved in
one turn of the price-wage spiral vanish in the next," as
President Kennedy pointed out in his 1962 *Economic Report*. As labor's "money illusion" fades, it sees more and
more clearly that the 1960–1965 advances of average take-

home pay by 21 percent in current dollars and 13 percent in constant dollars are not just one third better, but over three times as good as the 1955–1960 advances of 15 percent in current and 4 percent in constant dollars.

The *public* now has a better yardstick for determining whether particular wage and price decisions are economically defensible. It can more readily spot labor-management "collusion" on overgenerous wage boosts, the bill for which is passed along to the consumer in higher prices. And people are becoming more aware that their stake in wage-price decisions goes beyond the cost of living to the very heart of prosperity — that price and cost increases growing out of the market power of business and labor can undermine our international competitive position and force reversals of expansionary policy short of full employment. Guidepost debates also help to focus the spotlight on rising productivity as the key to higher wages and profits without higher prices.

All this is not to deny that the wage-price guideposts themselves walk an educational tightrope. On one hand, they clarify many issues and serve to mobilize public opinion and government persuasion to bring wage and price decisions of high-power labor and business units into closer conformity with competitive behavior — they are designed to produce the competitive result rather than interfere with it. On the other, some of the distinctions the guideposts make are too fine — and too close to the narrow edge of error — for the public to grasp. The public may infer that whenever market forces, competitive or otherwise, generate an "unreasonable" price increase, government should step in and stop it. People may not distinguish clearly between the "creeping admonitionism" of the guideposts and the hobnailed boots of direct controls. This is the risk one runs when government appeals for wage and price restraint go beyond empty clichés to specific standards of behavior.

But the risk has been well worth taking. Having wandered this deeply into the guidepost thicket, I should add this judgment: that in spite of their imperfections and the dents and scars they bear — in spite of their uneven application and their inability to provide a built-in allowance for increases in the cost of living — the guideposts have served us tolerably well, in three respects.

First, though they have been a poor instrument of consensus, they have been a good instrument of education.

Second, judged both by privately expressed opinions (and public cries of pain) of business and labor and by careful comparative studies of wage and cost trends, the guideposts can fairly take credit for some of the wage-price moderation in the great expansion of the 1960's.

Third, and this is in the "least evils" vein: Faced with the conflict between full employment and price stability — and recognizing that guideposts are no substitute for higher taxes and tight money to deal with demand-pull inflation — what would guidepost-haters have us do? Simply accept cost-push and price-push inflation? Impose wage and price ceilings? Hold wages and prices down by keeping the economy slack? Pulverize big business and big labor to destroy their discretionary power to set prices and wages? Merely to list these is to suggest, in Kermit Gordon's words, that "the policy contemplated in the wage-price guideposts — the one of education, persuasion, creation of a climate in the public mind designed to encourage exercise of long-run self-interest — seems the most acceptable." [38]

Microeconomic understanding. Although many of the issues in wage-price productivity relationships have been clarified in recent years, we have made no great leap forward in microeconomic understanding. The role and merits of the market system as an allocator of resources are, as I noted earlier, understood by economists but only hazily perceived by the public.

The great truths of macroeconomic policies for full employment and stability — even though they often seem to contradict the maxims of private finance — can be painted in broad brush strokes, dramatized, and even put in the pleasant form of fiscal dividends like tax cuts or Great Society programs. But the microeconomic elements of policy for growth and stability are, generally speaking, more subtle, less dramatic, and more forbidding.

Their subtlety is apparent. Their lack of drama seems to be contradicted by the high drama of the 1962 steel crisis and the 1965 facedown on aluminum prices. But these are rare exceptions. As far as public education is concerned, an event like the steel confrontation generates, not the light that illuminates, but the flash that blinds. And microeconomic policy more often calls for unpleasant restraints like guideposts and antitrust laws than for welcome stimulants like tax credits for investments.

Nor have educational efforts in the microeconomic field been buttressed by policy actions whose message was loud and clear, like the tax cut's clarion call to the macroeconomic colors. Indeed, the micro-policy message has been muffled and at times equivocal. Faced with institutional constraints that rule out ideal solutions, we have had to resort to stopgaps that interfere with the free play of market forces — temporarily, one hopes and assumes — in order to serve some of our supervening economic objectives.

For example, the search for balance-of-payments equilibrium in a context that rules out flexible exchange rates, devaluation, and a world central bank gives us the choice of (1) imposing unpalatable curbs like the tying of our foreign aid to U.S. goods and services (even when better bargains could be struck elsewhere) and restraining capital outflows by taxes and voluntary curbs — all bad microeconomics — or (2) purposely maintaining unemployment and slack in the U.S. economy with the aid of high interest rates — all bad macroeconomics — to discourage money outflows and imports and encourage money inflows and exports.

We have, wisely, I think, chosen the former route. But the resulting interference with market pricing and resource allocation, even if temporary, has its costs in reduced efficiency, freedom of choice, and effectiveness in implanting microeconomic truths. This requires redoubled efforts by Presidents and their advisers to distinguish sharply between our immediate objectives — overcoming our balance-of-payments deficits and further reducing our gold outflow

— and our ultimate goals of maintaining a reasonably free and efficient system of world commerce, finance, and production.

Not surprisingly, however, the main burden of government efforts to gain public understanding of microeconomic principles will fall on economic advisers rather than on Presidents. One can hardly expect Presidents to be drawn to the teaching of economic principles that are subtle, offer little drama, commonly involve — or seem to involve — low stakes and bitter pills, and periodically have to be honored in the breach rather than the observance.

As economic advisers, we found that Kennedy was in due course quite ready to speak out on the great issues of expansionary policy to restore full employment and step up growth. But when Kermit Gordon and I finally induced him, one day, to speak out on microeconomic matters — with emphasis on the role and merits of competitive enterprise, the pricing system, and profits — neither he nor his audience (the White House Conference of Business Editors and Publishers, September 26, 1962) seemed to find the subject very intriguing.

Yet, if we manage to solve tolerably well the macroeconomic problem of keeping the economy moving along the path of its noninflationary potential, both President and public will have no choice but to learn their microeconomic lessons. For then — apart from the ticklish job of timing and tuning fiscal-monetary policy to keep supply and demand in balance and to avoid the excesses that destroy expansions — we return to the classical problems of the fully employed economy. One claim on resources must come at the expense of others, and the microeconomic issues of efficient allocation come strongly to the fore.

This reminds us that even though the gulf between professional and popular economics is a good deal narrower than it was, the problem of economic communication will constantly change in form and focus and continue to be difficult and demanding. And the prickly dilemmas posed by inflation could bring setbacks to the public acceptance of the political economist and his wares. This could happen if those who have a vested intellectual or political interest in doing so manage to establish the 1964–65 tax cuts rather than Vietnam as the inflationary culprit — or scapegoat — in today's economy. Worse yet, if fiscal and monetary policies are consistently less vigorous in checking overexpansion than in combatting underexpansion, the resulting inflationary bias could in part discredit the "new economics." I say "consistently" because 1966 alone will not be a sufficient test: inflation has been mild; the economic dialogue has been kept on a high plane; the President and his advisers have stated the issues and the dangers quite plainly; and a substantial minority of informed opinion has felt that the degree of monetary-fiscal restriction applied was about right. But we still stand in need of wider understanding of the perils of high-pressure prosperity and a clearer demonstration that policy is prepared to meet them.

From this review of the vital role of education in the policy-making process, it should be apparent that Presidential economic advisers cannot wrap themselves in their professional cocoons and hope to be effective. Politics is often called the "art of the possible." The political economist who advises Presidents not only has to operate within the bounds of the possible but has to help the President push out those bounds.

This conclusion has a bearing on the fears of a "technician's take-over" which have been expressed by some observers of the governmental process. Bertrand de Jouvenel, for example, asserts that professional government can promote the general welfare, but cannot be made politically democratic.[39] But this seems to me to overlook that it is *only* by being responsive — by making their products marketable not merely to their Number One Customer, but to the Congress, the press, and the public — that professional advisers can get their message and their policies across.

No matter how inescapable the logic of the Keynesian idea may have been, and how apparent it was to economists as long as 20 or 25 years ago, it was not an "idea whose time had come" until it could be put in a form and framework which made it acceptable to the public and attractive to Presidents. That may not be economic optimality, but it *is* political democracy.

ADVISORY MACHINERY

An understanding of U.S. economic policy making and the professional adviser's place in it requires at least a brief review of the advisory machinery, the conduits through which advice flows to the President. My observations here will be centered on the CEA, which is "a professional but political economic arm of the presidency that has no counterpart in any other country." [40]

Other advanced countries typically couple the economic advisory function with a cluster of operating functions, assigning responsibility for both to an established agency in the hierarchy, even in the Cabinet. This is true of the new Ministry of Economic Affairs in Great Britain, the German Economic Ministry, and the French Ministry of Finance and Economics. They sit astride a flow of business that supports them from below. The Council of Economic Advisers, in contrast, is suspended from above. That may be their strength and CEA's weakness. But it is also CEA's strength and their weakness in that the Council is, and they are not, part of the Executive Office per se. This position in the scheme of things offers the advisers easy and direct access to the Chief Executive. And, in turn, it puts at his disposal a catholic, not a parochial, approach to economic policy — an undivided, rather than a competing, loyalty (though professional integrity *could* become a competitor).

The President knows that the Council's expertise is fully at his command, undiluted by the commitments to particular programs and particular interest groups that, in the nature of things, tend to build up in the various line agencies of government. So although no law and no hierarchical flow of business force a President to rely on the Council of Economic Advisers — not even the Employment Act, which places the Council at his disposal but does not require him to use it (except in preparation of his annual *Economic Report*) — it is his most natural ally in economic matters.

Yet, the Council's access to the President is potential, not guaranteed. Unless personalities click; unless the economic adviser is both right and relevant; unless he gets off of his academic high horse without falling obsequiously to the ground — his usefulness will be limited and his state of proximity to the President will gradually wither away.

My preoccupation with the Presidency will not have gone unnoticed. This concern is natural enough in an agency that is suspended, as I say, from above. It has no trouble generating plenty of busy-ness on its own, even if the President rarely calls. But it is the business with and for the President that makes the standard 80-to-90 hour week of Council members productive, rewarding, and memorable.

Access not just to the person but to the mind of the President is crucial. The Council's major instrument of access to a modern President is the development of economic concepts, targets, and policies that fit his philosophy and further his high purposes — indeed, sometimes give concrete shape to those purposes, as did the concepts of economic potential and the GNP gap and the targets of 4-percent unemployment and 4½-percent annual growth. All of these were imprinted with the Presidential seal in Kennedy's first year and thereby became Administration policy. As Tobin has observed, "It was of no small importance that the Council's definition and estimation of the targets of government policy under the Employment Act became Administration doctrine, adopted throughout the Executive Branch . . . Whether in inter-agency debate or in public discussion, it became difficult for government spokesmen to advocate policies that held no prospect of reaching the target in a reasonable time." [41]

The *Economic Report*, memoranda, general policy sessions with the President, Cabinet meetings, direct or indirect responsibility for Presidential messages and pronouncements all afford the economic adviser important opportunities to influence Administration economic policy. But in the early months of the Kennedy Administration, we found that on many specific decisions involving economic policy, the Council had become only a flag stop on the policy-making track. Unless the White House took a hand in directing economic traffic through the Council, the policy train often flashed past before we could get out the flag to stop it. One of our major tasks was to establish constructive relationships with the men around the President to help insure that the Council's voice would be heard before final decisions were made, even if it had not been drawn into the early stages of the policy-making process. The corridors to power in domestic affairs ran through the offices of people like Sorensen, O'Donnell, Ralph Dungan, and Lawrence O'Brien. Their confidence and their conviction that the Council had something important or even unique to offer to Presidential decision making were essential.

The Council relied on this relationship in particular for an opportunity to be heard on the economic implications of issues and programs outside the mainstream of economic policy for stability and growth. Examples that come to mind are housing programs and their financing, agricultural price supports, maritime subsidies, transportation regulations, social security benefits, and payroll tax increases. As the importance of this function became more evident, the Council was brought into the year-end legislative planning process in the White House to advise on the economic aspects of all phases of the President's domestic program, much as the Bureau of the Budget advises on the budgetary aspects.

Only as the network of relations within the Executive Office of the President, with White House assistants, and with Cabinet and sub-Cabinet members was gradually built could the Council feel that its position in the economic policy process was reasonably secure. As an alumnus of the Council, I can only hope that enough of a tradition is developing so that the process of reconstructing this network in another Administration one day will come rather more easily than it did to us. But tradition or no, the role of the Council will surely change from one Administration to the next, and its levers of power will have to be renewed and rebuilt each time there is a change of scene and a new cast of characters.

In spite of the somewhat uncertain and changing nature of the Council's role — resulting from its heavy dependence on the President's favor and its own ability to make itself useful — I do not favor buttressing its position with specific program responsibilities. I mention this because in the early days those who were advising Kennedy on the management of the Presidency wanted to assign the Council advisory functions in the fields of manpower and public works and consumer protection. Initially, this idea appealed to me. But experience soon convinced me that if the Council is to be put to its best uses in general policy advising, and if it is to maintain the compactness and flexibility that small size makes possible — it has a total staff of only forty, of whom fifteen are economists — such an enlargement of scope would be unwise. We had a test of this principle in the period when the Consumer Advisory Council was attached to the CEA. We found that this program, or operating, responsibility not only diverted energies and efforts from the Council's central purpose and competence but threatened to get it entangled in the conflicts and cross fire of special interest groups. The Council should stand above these.

Almost four years of service as Council chairman kindled in me no burning desire for changes in the formal organization of economic advice in the Federal government. After a year and a half's perspective on the matter as a nonparticipant, I have not changed my view. I do not see, for example, that a National Economic Council paralleling the National Security Council would serve an essential need which is now being neglected.

This conclusion is not a vote for no change in the economic advisory machinery, but a vote for fluidity. I do not contend that the present arrangements are the best of all worlds. Each President will recast the Council in his own image.[42] He will probably flank it with a "Troika" (an advisory group consisting of the Secretary of the Treasury, the Director of the Budget, and the Chairman of the CEA) or a "Quadriad" (the Troika plus the Chairman of the Federal Reserve Board), as both Presidents Kennedy and Johnson have done. Or perhaps he will prefer a quintet or sextet. When special policy situations call for a broader view, a President can turn to a special committee like the Cabinet Committee on Growth that President Kennedy set up in August 1962. It became an important vehicle for Administration consensus on the over-all dimensions of the tax cut.[43]

One subsidiary change in machinery may be desirable if a large flow of business develops under the wage-price guideposts, namely, to set up a separate wage-price unit independent in, but not of, the CEA. Guidepost questions and cases could be referred to this unit rather than to the Council itself, thus bringing two potential gains. First, the Council might thereby sidestep a role that *appears* to be political, no matter how objective and analytical it may be in fact. Second, as Gerhard Colm has suggested, it might give the Council a little relief from its fire-brigade pressures, a little more time for needed work on long-run problems.[44]

So far it may seem that I have been preoccupied with questions of power — the power of ideas, the power of Presidents, the power of economic advisers. And I have. But I make no apology. For I have been dealing with instrumental, not ultimate, power; with the instruments through which the capabilities of modern economics — to be consistent, I should say the power of positive economics — can be turned to the common good.

§ CHAPTER II § The Promise of Modern Economic Policy

The significance of the great expansion of the 1960's lies not only in its striking statistics of employment, income, and growth but in its glowing promise of things to come. If we can surmount the economic pressures of Vietnam without later being trapped into a continuing war on inflation when we should again be fighting economic slack, the "new economics" can move us steadily toward the qualitative goals that lie beyond the facts and figures of affluence.

In the last analysis, the promise of modern economic policy in a democracy lies in its capacity to serve our ultimate social objectives in a framework of freedom. That promise can be realized only if the government, first, carries out its responsibility under the Employment Act of 1946 to create and maintain the *conditions* for a thriving full-employment economy; second, does so by *means* that will reconcile rational government behavior in economic matters with decentralized decisions and freedom of economic choice; and, third, puts the products of prosperity and growth to *uses* that carry out a democratic society's aspirations not only for material betterment but for a rising quality of life and growing equality of opportunity.

The distinguishing feature of the "new economics" is not that it is new but that it has newly pressed into the public service the lessons of modern economics — of Keynes and the Classics — to help make good this promise. In this chapter I will be concerned with the objectives, working concepts, and policy content of the "new economics," its performance in both a slack and a taut economy, and what it demands of future policy and promises in return.

The Employment Act, the nation's economic Magna Carta, calls upon the Federal government — with the cooperation of industry, agriculture, labor, and state and local governments, and in ways that will promote free competitive enterprise — to use "all its plans, functions, and resources . . . to promote maximum employment, production, and purchasing power." [1] Through "judicious interpretation" under four Presidents, this mandate has gradually evolved into the four-dimensional objective of full employment, high growth, price stability, and balance-of-payments equilibrium[2] — sought within the constraints of growing equality of opportunity and freedom of choice.

Behind each of the four immediate economic objectives lie the more abiding social goals and values we cherish, the goals and values the "new economics" actively seeks to serve:

Full employment of our human and material resources. The term "full employment" stands as a proxy, as it were, for the fulfillment of the individual as a productive member of society, for the greater equality that grows out of giving every able-bodied worker access to a job, and for a national determination to demonstrate that a market economy, based on freedom of choice, *can* make full and productive use of its great potential.

• *Rapid economic growth,* our proxy for a rising standard and quality of life at home, and an ever-broadening base for our economic and political leadership abroad.

• *Price stability,* our proxy for equity between fixed and variable income recipients and, in today's outward-looking economy, a vital condition for maintaining our competitive position in world markets without trade restriction.

• *Balance-of-payments equilibrium,* our proxy for promoting an international economic setting in which there will be free movement of people, commerce, and finance across national boundaries, and free scope for expansionary domestic policies.

THE PRELUDE TO POLICY

Even after the national purpose is expressed in proximate aims, these aims must be translated into meaningful operational concepts and quantitative targets not only to meet the requirements of the Employment Act but to give decision makers the concrete standards they need to gauge performance, prescribe policy, and periodically reset our economic thermostats. Each of these needs calls for comment.

The language of the Employment Act is explicit, even if inelegant, in requiring the President to set forth "the levels of employment, production, and purchasing power obtaining in the United States and such levels needed to carry out the policy" of the act, together with "current and foreseeable economic trends" in these levels.[8] These provisions calling for quantitative targets and forecasts had lain virtually dormant for some years when President Kennedy, late in 1960, gave them new life with his call to "return to the spirit as well as the letter of the Employment Act" and "to deal not only with the state of the economy but with our goals for economic progress." [4]

But even if the act had not required quantitative targets, activist policy does. Without them, how can the decision maker aim at finite economic objectives and make hard choices among alternatives, as he must? Presidents need to know — to the best of their economists' ability — how high they can push employment and output with reasonable price stability. If, for example, we had followed the advice of those who urged us to fix our job sights on a 5-percent rather than a 4-percent level of unemployment, it would have automatically lowered our GNP target by $20 billion. The resulting signal for tax reduction would have called for a cut of only $4 billion in 1964 instead of nearly $12 billion.

Standards of economic performance must be recast from time to time. Recasting them in more ambitious terms was an indispensable prelude to the shaping of economic policies for the 1960's which would be suitable to the tremendous output capabilities of the U.S. economy.

In 1961, once recession had turned into recovery, nothing was more urgent than to raise the sights of economic policy and to shift its focus from the ups and downs of the cycle to the continuous rise in the economy's potential.

Policy emphasis had to be redirected from a *corrective* orientation geared to the dynamics of the cycle, to a *propulsive* orientation geared to the dynamics and the promise of growth.[5] For this purpose, it was essential that the Council of Economic Advisers formulate specific, usable models within which to relate prognosis and prescription, economic targets and economic policies.

The main instrument for dethroning the cyclical model and enthroning the growth model has been the *GNP* or *performance gap* and the associated estimates of the economy's potential and growth rate at 4-percent unemployment ("full" or "high" employment). These guides have now passed the rugged test of five years' use as benchmarks for policies to match demand with capacity, culminating in the virtual closing of the gap as the economy reached and broke through the 4-percent unemployment level early in 1966.

Estimating the trend rate of growth for this purpose was a comparatively unemotional — if technically intricate — matter of adding together the growth rates in labor inputs and productivity. When we initiated the "official" calculation in 1961, this growth in potential was running at a rate of 3½ percent a year; it is now nearly 4 percent.

But setting an employment target and relating it to a firm estimate of the U.S. economy's output potential were much more difficult and emotionally charged matters. Consider the setting — the unemployment rate was close to 7 percent of the labor force. It had been above 4 percent for four straight years. It had risen in each of the three successive business cycle peaks of the 1950's and had stayed above 5 percent at the peak of the anemic recovery in 1960. Talk of "structural unemployment" was loose in the land — indeed, very loose.

The structural-unemployment thesis — the proposition that there had been a great *increase* in hard-core unemployment which would not yield to demand stimulus — found supporters from every point on the political spectrum. Automation supposedly had us by the throat. There was a great mismatch between the skills demanded and the skills that could be supplied. If we set our employment target too high and tried to achieve it with tax cuts or other fiscal stimulants to demand, we would simply be trying to pound square pegs into round holes. The results would be bottlenecks and inflation, not higher output and more jobs.

Anyone who couldn't see that, we were told, was blind. The ravages of automation were obvious: displaced elevator operators, oil refinery workers, telephone operators, even assembly-line workers. Were servo-mechanisms really taking over? Or were people falling prey to Albert G. Hart's "Law of Observation," namely, that in a country as large as the United States, you can find fifty examples of anything?

Careful analyses of the statistical record within CEA convinced us that the structural-unemployment thesis was more fancy than fact, since the structural component of unemployment had *not* risen;[6] that the 4-percent unemployment target was not only attainable but should be viewed as an interim target, later to be reset at a lower level (after manpower programs had increased labor skills and mobility); and that we had a sound method of translating the employment goal into a GNP target and thus defining the gap between actual and potential GNP.[7]

The reactions to the 4-percent figure — both from those who thought it too high and from those who thought it too low — removed any illusions I might have had about political economy being able to abstract from values and emotions. On one side, we were condemned as heartless for setting a goal, even an interim goal, that would leave three million people unemployed. On the other, we were assailed as reckless for believing we could drive the economy that far without colliding with structural barriers and bringing on a rash of inflation. Employment developments in 1965–66 rendered a clear-cut verdict on the structural-unemployment thesis: the alleged hard core of unemployment lies not at 5 or 6 percent, but even deeper than 4 percent — how deep still remains to be ascertained.

THE NEW LOOK IN FISCAL POLICY

Reorienting policy targets and strategy to the economy's full and growing potential yielded not only new norms but new semantics for stabilization policy, especially in its fiscal aspects.

Gap-closing and growth. This, rather than the smoothing of the business cycle became the main preoccupation of policy, its broader guide to action. As we put it in our January 1962 *Annual Report:* "The mandate of the Employment Act renews itself perpetually as maximum levels of production, employment, and purchasing power rise through time. The weapons of stabilization policy — the budget, the tax system, control of the supply of money and credit — must be aimed anew, for their target is moving." [8]

Fiscal drag. The moment the upward-moving target was recognized, three things became clear.

First, the traditional thinking that tended to identify prosperity with a rising economy often gave the wrong signals to fiscal policy, calling for a cut-off of its stimulus long before the production gap was closed, long before full employment was reached. Part of the critical barrage that greeted Kennedy's tax-cut proposal early in 1963 was based on this failure to distinguish between the *direction* of the economy, which was up, and its *level*, which was still far below its capabilities.

Second, the vaunted "built-in flexibility" of our tax system, its automatic stabilizing effect, is a mixed blessing. True, it cushions recessions, which is good. But left to its own devices it also retards recovery by cutting into the growth of private income, which is bad — at least until the production gap is closed and inflation threatens.

Third, in a growth context, the great revenue-raising power of our Federal tax system produces a built-in average increase of $7 to $8 billion a year in Federal revenues (net of the automatic increase in transfer payments). Unless it is offset by such "fiscal dividends" as tax cuts or expansion of Federal programs, this automatic rise in revenues will become a "fiscal drag" siphoning too much of the economic substance out of the private economy and thereby choking expansion.[9]

Fiscal dividends. A central part of the job of fiscal policy is precisely this delicate one of declaring fiscal dividends of the right size and timing to avoid fiscal drag without inviting inflation. In an overheated economy, the fiscal drag that develops when fiscal dividends are *not* declared is a welcome antidote to inflation. When recession threatens, an extra dividend is appropriate. But in normal times we must close the fiscal loop by matching the annual $7 to $8 billion of revenue growth with tax cuts, increased expenditures (including social security benefits), and more generous support to state and local governments.

Full-employment (or high-employment) surplus. As part of the reshaping of stabilization policy, then, our fiscal-policy targets have been recast in terms of "full" or "high" employment levels of output, specifically the level of GNP associated with a 4-percent rate of unemployment. So the target is no longer budget balance every year or over the cycle, but balance (in the national-income-accounts, or NIA, budget) at full employment. And in modern stabilization policy, as we will see in a moment, even this target does not remain fixed.

To know that the actual budget deficit in 1961 (NIA basis) was $3.8 billion tells us very little about the economic impact of the budget. We cannot tell whether it was expansionary or restrictive, and by how much. Even when we know that $3.8 billion represented a swing of about $7 billion from 1960, when the budget ran a surplus of $3.5 billion, we are not much better off. How much of this swing was the automatic result of changes in output and income? How much was the purposive result of changes in fiscal policy? We don't know. But if we put both years on a comparable basis — specifically, at the GNP levels that would yield our target level of 4-percent unemployment — we can immediately judge how big a burden the economy was carrying in its struggle to get back to full employment, and how much of that burden was being removed by conscious fiscal action.

So we have adopted as our fiscal gauge the "full employment surplus," the excess of revenues over expenditures which would prevail at 4-percent unemployment. It lifts the veil to tell us that the budget in 1961 would have been running a surplus of about $10 billion at full, or high, employment. It tells us also that Federal fiscal action had brought that surplus down from a huge $13 billion in 1960. What on its face looked like a stimulative budget in 1961 was, in fact, still exerting a strong fiscal drag on the economy in spite of the removal of about $3 billion of that drag through Federal fiscal action.[10]

Although our budget policy of recent years has been aimed at approximate balance at full employment, there are times when we may want to shift its target to a surplus or deficit, depending on the underlying strength of demand, the stimulative or restrictive effect of monetary policy, and so on. The large swings in the strength of private demand in the postwar period serve to remind us that the targets of compensating government policy have to shift correspondingly. The $13 billion full-employment surplus in 1960 was an oppressive economic drag, a major force pulling us down into the recession of 1960–61. Yet a big surplus in the face of surging postwar demand in the late 1940's — at a time when we had tied our monetary-policy hands behind our backs — represented, not fiscal oppression, but a welcome restraint on inflation.

In other words, the long period of slack private demand relative to the economy's potential after 1957 should not lead us to the conclusion that it will be ever thus. As fears of recession, properly, win less of a role in the businessman's investment calculus and the consumer's saving calculus, both investment and consumption propensities may shift upward. If so, the fiscal-policy targets should shift upward to a significant full-employment surplus. A changing fiscal-monetary mix could have the same implication. Monetary policy may one day be able to shift from its 1961–1965 role of accommodating a fiscally spurred expansion as best it could in the face of the conflicting demands of balance-of-payments policy — or its 1965–66 role of damping demands through tight money — to a post-Vietnam role of promoting growth through lower interest rates and easier money. When that day comes, the possibility of combining tighter fiscal policy (a full-employment surplus) with easier money will be back on the stabilization-policy agenda.

Operationally, training our sights on specified full-employment targets led to several significant changes in fiscal strategy.

First, it became more activist and bolder. Feeding fiscal stimulus into a briskly rising economy — typified by the Berlin defense buildup without a tax increase in 1961 and, even more, by the huge tax cut in 1964 — is now seen as a prudent response to the needs of an expanding economy that is still operating well below its full potential.

Second, it follows that fiscal strategy has to rely less on the automatic stabilizers and more on discretionary action responding to observed and forecast changes in the economy — less on rules and more on men.[11]

Third, under the new approach, not only monetary policy but fiscal policy has to be put on constant, rather than intermittent, alert. Since 1961, there have been almost continuous official consideration and public debate over tax cuts and expenditure increases to stimulate the economy or, since late 1965, tax increases or expenditure cuts to curb inflation. Clearly, the management of prosperity is a full-time job.

In part, this shift from a more passive to a more active policy has been made possible by steady advances in fact-gathering, forecasting techniques, and business practice. Our statistical net is now spread wider and brings in its catch faster. Forecasting has the benefit of not only more refined, computer-assisted methods, but of improved surveys of consumer and investment intentions. And the advances made in strategic planning and systematic analysis in business are building a better base for forecasting the inventory and capital-spending sector of the GNP.

At the same time, the margin for error diminishes as the economy reaches the treasured but treacherous area of full employment. Big doses of expansionary medicine were easy — and safe — to recommend in the face of a $50 billion gap and a hesitant Congress. But at full employment, targets have to be defined more sharply, tolerances are smaller, the line between expansion and inflation becomes thinner. So in a full employment world the economic dosage has to be much more carefully controlled, the premium on quantitative scientific knowledge becomes far greater, and the premium on speed in our fiscal machinery also rises. As I shall discuss later, our fiscal processes have not yet caught up with our advances in fiscal policy. In spite of the rapid responses to President Johnson's tax requests in 1965 and 1966, congressional tax machinery is not yet speedy enough to meet the economic needs of the times.

THE "NEW ECONOMICS" AT WORK, 1961–1965

Within the foregoing framework of objectives and standards, economic policy moved at first haltingly and then dramatically into the new world of Keynes-cum-growth. Most of the observers of the 1961–1965 experience under the new economic policy have focused on the workings and wonders of the 1964 tax cut. Not that it didn't work or that it wasn't wonderful. But I think we have overdone the tax-cut story a bit. To get a balanced view, we must look beyond tax cuts to expenditure increases, and beyond fiscal stimulants and expansion of demand to the companion structural measures designed to increase productivity and maintain price stability.

If 1961–1965 policy had been as one-track-minded about expansion as casual critics often picture it, it would stand us in poor stead today. It was only because economic policy gave equal billing to measures for higher productivity and cost-price stability that *sustained* growth was made possible.

POLICIES FOR DEMAND EXPANSION

To get a bird's-eye view of five years of expansionary fiscal policy, perhaps the best way is to observe how the Federal government deployed $48 billion of fiscal dividends (at annual rates) between the second half of 1960 and the second half of 1965. This huge figure embraces not only the offsetting, or absorption, of the $34 billion by which high-employment revenues would have grown if Federal tax rates had stayed at their 1960 levels, but also the wiping out of the $14 billion high-employment surplus that existed late in 1960.

The forms of fiscal dividends in this period were as follows (in billions of dollars, rounded):[12]

Tax Reductions		*Expenditure Increases*	
Personal income tax	$11	Defense and space purchases	$11
Corporate income tax	6	Personal transfer payments	9
Excise tax	2	Grants-in-aid	5
Payroll tax		Interest and subsidy payments	4
(*increase*)	–3	Domestic nondefense purchases	3
Net tax reduction	$16	Expenditure increases	$32

Tax cuts of $19 billion, less $3 billion of payroll tax increases, were the major form of dividend. They dwarfed the discretionary increases in Federal civilian expenditures, consisting mainly of the $3 billion of domestic nondefense purchases and a small fraction of the transfer, interest, and subsidy payments. Defense and space, plus automatic increases in interest, social security benefits, and grants-in-aid, accounted for the lion's share of the increase in Federal spending.

Thus, the big income tax cut in 1964 ($14 billion at 1965, $11 billion at 1963, income levels) is rightfully regarded as the most overt and dramatic expression of the new approach to economic policy. The successful use of the GNP gap and full-employment surplus in fixing the size of the 1964 tax cut deserves brief comment.

The production, or GNP, gap, which had narrowed from about $50 billion in early 1961 to $30 billion in early 1962 — and then held stubbornly at that level — was instrumental in setting the proposed net tax cut at roughly $11 billion. On the basis of observed stable relationships between disposable income and consumption, together with not-so-stable investment relationships, the Administration spelled out how the proposed cut would multiply itself into an increment of GNP that could "close or nearly close, the gap between potential and actual output . . ." [13] The tax cut was also designed to bring the high-employment surplus — which had been reduced to $6½ billion in 1962 but grew to over $11 billion (by the end of 1963) while Congress was debating the tax cut — down to, or close to, zero.

Thus the rationale of the 1964 tax-cut proposal came straight out of the country's postwar economics textbooks. And in turn the tax cut itself — recently described by Dexter Keezer as "a triumph of high-test Keynesian economic therapy" [14] — will richly repay its debt to the textbooks by supplying the classic example of modern fiscal policy and multiplier economics at work. Careful appraisal of the tax cut's impact on GNP shows a remarkably close fit of results to expectations.[15] And until Vietnam intervened, the tax cut *had* brought us back to a "balanced budget in a balanced economy" — in fact, by the first half of 1965, Federal receipts had already risen $7½ billion above their pre-tax-cut levels, and the Federal budget (NIA basis) was in surplus. So in conception as in delivery, it was a textbook tax cut.

POLICIES FOR PRODUCTIVITY AND COST-PRICE STABILITY

The 1964 tax cut captured the public's attention and imagination and led to a profound change in public attitudes. Its expansionary melody was quickly and easily learned. Taxpayers were still humming the happy tune in 1965 when nearly $5 billion of excise tax cuts were enacted.

But the harmonics of economic policy for cost-price stability are more subtle and less readily committed to memory. Yet they are equally important — they are a co-requisite of sustained prosperity. The discouraging pattern of recessions every two or three years between 1949 and 1960 has been broken, not by a simple-minded devotion to demand stimulus, but by a tight coupling of measures to boost demand with measures to boost productivity and hold costs in check — a combination designed to bring the demands of full employment into harmony with those of high growth, cost-price stability, and external payments equilibrium.

Indeed, sizable and sustained productivity advances may be thought of as "the great reconciler." From 1961 to 1965, rapidly rising output per unit of input made it possible largely to satisfy the rising income claims of business and labor while holding, or even cutting, unit costs of output.

Moderation in wages and prices becomes more bearable
when higher productivity, bigger volume, and lower taxes
keep take-home pay and profits rising merrily.

The search for ways and means to build a firm base of
price-cost stability for expansion began in 1961, long before
massive tax stimulants to demand were proposed. A first
line of defense against inflation had been provided by the
legacy of price stability that grew out of the restrictive
monetary-fiscal policies, economic slack, high unemployment, and slow growth that ushered in the 1960's. But the
hard task was to maintain that stability while stimulating
the economy, taking up the slack, restoring full employment, and doubling the rate of growth. To accomplish it
required several important innovations in American economic policy.

Tax stimulants to investment. Most important among the
measures to speed the advances of productivity were $3
billion of tax incentives to investment in plant and equipment recommended in April 1961 and put into effect in
1962. Added to these were another $3 billion of corporate
tax rate deductions in 1964. The combination of investment
tax credits, more liberal depreciation, and lower corporate
rates may be thought of as a $6 billion shift from public to
private saving, one that offered direct investment stimulants
in the form of expanded cash flows as well as increased
profitability of investment projects.

Manpower training and retraining measures. Measures to
stimulate physical investment in plant and equipment were
accompanied by increased intangible investments in human
beings. Manpower development and retraining measures

initiated early in 1961 were the forerunners of a long line of programs — including new aids to education and large segments of the war on poverty — which were designed to increase the skills, the quality, and the mobility of the labor force.

The monetary "twist." Another 1961 innovation was the effort to twist the structure of interest rates so as to hold down the costs of long-term funds for investment in new plant and equipment while raising short-term rates to minimize the outflows of volatile funds to other countries. Successive increases in interest rates payable by commercial banks on time deposits played an important role in redirecting the flow of funds from the short to the longer term end of the spectrum and thus serving the objectives of the twist. Only as the economy began to heat up under the impact of Vietnam was the twist dropped as part of a general monetary tightening to curb overexpansion.

Wage-price guideposts. This American counterpart to the "incomes policies" of Europe was introduced early in 1962. Since I have examined the guideposts at length in the first chapter, I will limit myself here to only two summary points. First, the guideposts have been a useful moderating influence in 1961–1965. Second, since they are designed to function as a supplement rather than an alternative to overall fiscal monetary policy, they should not be expected to carry the burden of stabilization — nor should they be judged by the performance of wages and prices — in a period of excessive total demand.

Other public policies. Among other steps taken in recent years to strengthen the structure and productive capacity

of the American economy are the programs to speed the
development of lagging regions; programs to step up scientific research and to improve civilian technology; and various efforts to modernize the Federal regulation of industry.

The contribution of private policy. Although my focus
here is on public policies, a vital factor not only in the
length and strength, but particularly in the balance and
moderation, of the great expansion of the 1960's has been
the impact of effective private policies — better inventory
and cost control, less speculation, better matching of plant
capacity to markets, and more restrained wage-price policies than we have had in any previous expansion in U.S.
history.

THE ECONOMIC RECORD [16]

That these public and private policies met their mark is
confirmed by our unmatched record of price and cost stability in the first half of this decade. The rise of only 1.3 percent a year in U.S. consumer prices from 1960 to 1965 —
and of only 2 percent in wholesale prices for the entire
period — is a record no other industrial nation can match.
Western European prices, for example, went up two to
three times as fast as ours.

The record also shows that from 1960 to 1965, average
unit-labor costs in the private economy rose by only 0.6
percent a year, less than one third as rapidly as the rise of
2.1 percent a year from 1953 to 1957, and less than one
half the 1.4 percent rise between 1957 and 1960. Unit labor
costs in manufacturing actually fell slightly between 1960

and 1965 as output per man-hour rose by an average of 4 percent annually while hourly compensation rose only 3.6 percent.

In weighing this evidence of stability, one must view it in the light of the remarkable advances in output, jobs, and income in the first five years of expansion (specifically, from the first quarter of 1961 to the first quarter of 1966). Gross national product advanced by $218 billion, or by one third in real terms. Over 7 million added jobs were created, bringing the unemployment rate down from nearly 7 percent to under 4 percent. Real per capita income, after taxes, rose by one fifth. The realized growth rate of the economy doubled, rising from 2¼ percent for the period 1953–1960 (measured from cyclical peak to cyclical peak) to 4½ percent since 1960.

Even more impressive, in a sense, are the great gains in the profits of business and the wages of labor resulting from the combination of rising productivity, higher sales volume, and lower taxes. Thus, corporate profits after taxes doubled between the first quarters of 1961 and 1966. At the same time (December 1960, to December 1965, to be exact), total real compensation of all employees, corrected for price increases, rose about 30 percent. The weekly take-home pay of the average manufacturing worker rose 18 percent, in contrast with a drop of 1 percent in the preceding five-year period.[17] In relative terms, labor held its own until 1965, when total compensation of employees was just over 70 percent of national income — almost unchanged from 1960 and 3 percent higher than 1955. (However, from mid-1965 on, as

profits continued to rise briskly while wage payments rose
no faster than the cost of living, some slippage took place
in labor's position.)

As we appraise our five-year experience with the double-
track policy of the "new economics" — one track leading
toward higher demand and production, the other, toward
higher productivity and cost-price stability — we have to
contend with critics who imply that if the economic pressures of Vietnam were to knock our expansion off balance,
it would discredit the policy experience of the entire period.
But lest they forget, as they now say, "I told you so," they
first told us so nearly five years and over $200 billion of
GNP ago, 7 million jobs and $25 billion of corporate profits
ago! I say this, of course, without rancor.

Yet I would remind the critics — men of high repute but
limited faith in the power and flexibility of the U.S. economy — that fairly early in 1961 they told us that the economy would reach full employment by the fall of 1962
without further government stimulus, indeed, that such
stimulus would simply run off in inflation. It didn't. Late
in 1962 they told us that a $2½ billion tax cut was all the
economy could stand, that a tax cut of several times that
amount was not only unorthodox but bizarre, and would
generate "simply enormous deficits." It didn't. Late in 1963
the critics told us that structural unemployment — com-
pounded by automation — would frustrate the expansionary impact of the tax cut and bring inflation long before the
4-percent unemployment target was reached. It didn't. And
in 1964 we were warned that too big a tax cut, coupled with

too little tax withholding in 1964, would overheat the economy in 1964 and cool it off early in 1965. It didn't.

THE DECLINE OF THE DOCTRINAIRE

But the record of the 1961–1966 experience in putting modern economics to work is not to be read solely in the statistics of sustained expansion or in critics confounded. An important part of the story is a new flexibility in the economic thinking of both liberals and conservatives. Both have been dislodged from their previously entrenched positions, their ideological foxholes, by the force of economic circumstance and the impact of policy success.

Among the interlocking shifts in liberal Democratic policy in the early 1960's was the increased emphasis on investment relative to consumption, on tax cuts relative to expenditure increases, on cost-price stability relative to demand expansion, and on international relative to domestic considerations. What inference are we to draw from these changes in emphasis? That a government or leaders of a party have learned the error of their ways and are now on the path of eternal truth? Hardly. That a major political party has moved from left to right, from a labor to a business orientation, simply substituting a new dogma for an old?

On the contrary, it is an escape from dogma. It is a realization that, in President Kennedy's words, "What is at stake in our economic decisions today is, not some grand warfare of rival ideologies which will sweep the country with passion, but the practical management of a modern economy." [18]

And practical management, in turn, requires flexibility in attitudes and policy. On the one hand, it calls for a willingness to change priorities among multiple economic objectives, to respond to secular shifts in the strength or composition of demand, to adjust policy to the growing exposure of the economy to international economic forces. On the other, it calls for readiness to shift policy from expansion to restriction and back again in response to the changing strength of private demand and the changing size of public budgets.

The shift from consumption to investment stimulus is a case in point. As already suggested, the Kennedy Administration recognized from the outset that it could not hope to achieve its objectives of faster growth, stable prices, and a shrinking payments deficit without stepping up investment in plant and equipment. To modernize, mechanize, and automate, to translate advanced technology into actual output — this was essential not only to achieve faster growth but, even more pressing, to cut costs, keep prices stable, and improve our international competitive position. Yet, in the face of these needs, business fixed investment had dropped from about 11 percent of GNP early in the postwar period to roughly 9 percent after 1957. The clear answer, though un-Democratic in tradition, was to offer special tax incentives for investment in machinery and equipment.

The business community greeted the shift toward investment emphasis — coming from a liberal Democratic administration — with unhealthy skepticism. First, there was doubt that the Kennedy Administration would match its kind words for investment and profits with action. Second, there was suspicion about the form of the action, the "new-fangled" investment credit, a 7-percent tax credit for capital outlays on machinery and equipment. Third, when action came, businessmen expressed serious doubts about how much help it would actually give them in financing new investments. But skepticism soon vanished. In 1966, when some of us proposed to suspend the investment credit temporarily — to declare a Vietnam moratorium on the credit during the excessive capital goods boom — business put a big "no trespassing" sign on the investment credit. One can be pardoned, I hope, for seeing a strong parallel in the reactions of the young couple who were wheeling their baby buggy through the park: When the young mother gasped, "John, that's not our baby!" he came back with, "Shhh! It's a better buggy."

With great sea changes in long-run policy emphasis, then, one must couple flexibility in response to short-run fluctuations. Emphasis on high levels of investment — not only in plant and equipment, but in brainpower and research — is here to stay. It is essential to the economic growth and well-being of the nation. But we also have to recognize that too-rapid expansion of capital goods production can generate inflation and undermine our international competitive position, as it did in the 1955–1957 period, and that it can create overcapacity, as it did in the 1920's. Extremism in the pursuit of productivity through private capital spending can be a vice, at least temporarily. To distinguish between economic vice and economic virtue and adjust policy accordingly is absolutely essential for balanced economic expansion.

Fine distinctions and flexible adjustments in economic policy will come more readily as understanding deepens and consensus broadens. And here there are grounds for optimism. For matching the shift in the liberal or Democratic position has been a profound shift in the conservative position. Its chief characteristics are, first, a growing acceptance of government's essential role in the active use of fiscal-monetary policy for management of prosperity — and I use the word "management" advisedly — and, second, a growing understanding that such management need not destroy, endanger, or in any way limit individual freedom of choice.

A related bonus from recent policy experience is a steady ebbing of the unfounded fears that so often in the past caused our economic policy to be "sicklied o'er with the pale cast of thought." In particular, the fear that budget deficits necessarily spell inflation, insolvency, and irresponsibility has been refuted by the facts. Indeed, with respect to the public fisc, people increasingly see the wisdom of Artemus Ward's dictum that we should "all be happy and live within our means, even if we have to borrow the money to do it with." Another diminishing fear is that our national debt will burden our children and grandchildren and bring on national bankruptcy. Coupled with better understanding is the reassurance brought by the steady shrinkage of the debt as a proportion of GNP — from 118 percent in 1947 to 58 percent in 1960 to less than 45 percent in 1966.

Finally, the experience with the tax cut, in particular, is helping to allay the fear that fiscal planning, however prudent, necessarily spells growing centralization of power in Washington.

The success of expansionary policy, then, especially in the form of the tax cut, has undermined the position and thinned the ranks of the dug-in doctrinaire on both the left and the right. Minds have opened, and the area of common ground has grown. Doubters, disbelievers, and dissenters remain. Some vaguely feel it's "too good to be true." Others cling to beliefs too long cherished to flee before mere facts. But they are increasingly outside the main body of economic policy consensus.

This is not to say that we are on the threshold of the millennium in economic thinking. James MacGregor Burns need never fear — within this heartening growth of consensus, there is still plenty of room for creative tension, dissent, and conflict.[19]

THE "NEW ECONOMICS" IN HIGH-PRESSURE PROSPERITY

Yesterday's milestones do not solve today's problems, nor tomorrow's. In 1966 — partly as a penalty for the past successes of expansionary policy, but even more, as a result of war in Vietnam — the "new economics" has had to run the gauntlet of high-pressure prosperity. It has been brought face to face with this critical question: Can we manage that prosperity without a price-wage spiral? If we can, we will have reached a goal that has hitherto eluded not only this

The Promise of

country but all of its industrial partners in the free world.

The 1966 experience may not provide a clear-cut answer, but its illustrative value is great — it serves to clarify the issues and the dilemmas of political economy under the pressure of full employment. At the outset, one should note that the unexpectedly strong surge in real GNP in 1966 (advancing at an annual rate of 5½ percent) underscores again that this country, with its prodigious productive capacity, faces no runaway inflation, no breakaway price-wage spiral. At the same time it should be clear that a huge output potential alone does not prevent imbalances, distortions, cost-push pressures, or excessive demand. Only alert and intelligent economic policy — and a generous measure of good planning and good luck — can do that.

So 1966 put the economic practitioner to his severest test: having helped persuade both President and public that he could plot the path to well-paced expansion in an under-employed economy, he now faced the far more intricate and difficult task of reconciling full prosperity with price stability. He had to make a convincing case that modern economics must work both ways — that the pleasures of fiscal dividends and easy money to boost demand and generate jobs in a slack economy must at times give way to the pains of tighter money and higher taxes to take the inflationary strain out of a taut economy. Politically, he had to paddle his policy canoe upstream.

Yet the dilemma of political economy in 1966 has been not only political but economic. Let us assume that a nation which has accepted the idea of tax cuts to overcome slack, to close a "deflationary gap," would understand tax increases to cool off an overheating economy, to close an "inflationary gap." (The echoes of World War II and Korean War economics in that phrase remind us that Keynes is not entirely a newcomer to the firing line in Washington.) That still left the economic adviser with the hard task of determining whether the pressures would be strong enough — and sustained enough — to call for more than just taking the foot off the gas. Would it also require stepping on the brake, and, if so, how hard?

THE CHANGED POLICY SETTING

That economic policy had to change direction — from expansion to restriction — was quickly recognized once the costs of war in Vietnam became apparent late in 1965 and early in 1966. President Johnson promptly called for a reversal of automobile and telephone excise-tax cuts, for a sharp speedup in corporate tax payments, and for the introduction of graduated income tax withholding. The Congress responded quickly. The requested changes were law by mid-March. The President also pruned back his planned Great Society programs and slowed their rate of expansion.

Meanwhile, the Federal Reserve System had already put its foot on the monetary brake. During most of the expansion monetary policy had played a largely permissive role. Constrained by the balance-of-payments problem, it nonetheless served the cause of expansion by meeting the growing credit needs of the economy at no more than gently rising long-term borrowing costs. Close and friendly cooperation between monetary and fiscal authorities was the order of the day in the 1961–1965 expansion. But in December 1965, as overexpansion increasingly threatened, the Federal Reserve Board slipped out of the harness of monetary-fiscal coordination to raise the rediscount rate and touch off a wave of interest-rate increases. The Administration, although wincing at the timing and the "go-it-alone" nature of the action, did not seriously contest its substance.

But even after the shift in the direction of policy, the debate swirled around how far to go. Specifically, it focused on a temporary income tax increase. The growing maturity of national thinking was reflected in calls — not only from economists but from many business leaders — for an income tax increase of perhaps $4 to $5 billion, generally cast in the form of a 5 or 6 percent temporary surtax on individual and corporate income taxes.

One should pause a moment to reflect on the striking shift that had taken place in the policy setting. Just before the escalation in Vietnam in July 1965 many observers of the U.S. economic scene were expressing doubts about our ability to sustain prosperity into 1966. Their statements spoke of a "leveling out in the economy," of "a new period of slower growth" that might wind up in recession, and of the indications that "the nation's longest peacetime business expansion looks ready to take a breather." The possibility of a modest 1966 tax cut as an economic stimulant was being actively considered.

Yet within six months we were dealing with the overstimulus of Vietnam. One could point out that even with Vietnam defense outlays were still below 8 percent of GNP, far below the 13 percent level of the Korean War. But this tended to conceal the important economic fact that the rate of defense spending had jumped by $5 billion from mid-1965 to early 1966. Careful estimates of the indirect effects of both actual outlays and military contracts on inventories, plant and equipment spending, and consumption indicated that the added impact of Vietnam had been multiplied into something over $15 billion of current demand in the U.S. economy by the first quarter of 1966.

From these figures one wistfully concludes that, were it not for Vietnam, early 1966 would have found us comfortably contemplating the form and size of the fiscal dividends needed to keep us on the road to full employment, rather than considering what further actions might be needed to ease the strain on our productive capacity and deal with the vexing and perplexing problem of inflation. The political economist was confronted not only with the difficult technical question of how much demand pressure would be exerted, and how the economy would respond to it, but with some particularly troublesome questions of social priorities and values which would have to be weighed in the policy decision.

The main issue arose from the need — since unemployment had been brought down to its interim goal of 4 percent — to make the critical value choice between possible inflation and distortion on the one hand and more employment on the other. If unemployment were allowed to fall to 3 percent, we would extend employment opportunities deep into the work force. The steady fall in the unemployment rate in 1965–66 had especially benefited those groups which find it hardest to get jobs. A continued drop would further melt the barriers to employment for the unskilled, the nonwhite, the very young, and the very old in our work force.

Before taking restrictive action, then, one had to be quite sure that the risks and costs of inflation warranted foregoing such employment gains. What are these costs? In other words what was at stake, if policy steps were too little and too late — if the 3- to 4-percent rate of rise in the price level we were experiencing early in 1966 continued or accelerated? Part of the cost would be in economic discrimination against fixed income groups and adverse effects on our competitive position in world trade. But beyond that, accelerating inflation could eventually force us into either (1) sharply restrictive action that could derail the economy from its full-employment, high-growth track or (2) direct wage and price controls that would involve a huge price in inefficiency, inequity, and lost freedom of decision. And failure to hold inflation in check might undermine the growing confidence in positive economic policy.

STRIKING AN ECONOMIC BALANCE

President Johnson recognized both the risks and the remedies when he said, early in 1966, "If it should turn out that additional insurance [against inflation] is needed, then I am convinced that we should levy higher taxes rather than accept inflation — which is the most unjust and capricious form of taxation." [20]

But the economic calculus was clouded by uncertainty. One did not have to be a Cassandra to argue that the disquieting signs of too much demand were already clear enough early in 1966 to call for further restrictive action like a moderate tax increase. Nor did one have to be a Pollyanna to say that the economy, all things considered, had rolled remarkably well with the punch of Vietnam, that we should try to walk the economic tightrope without a tax increase — that perhaps the tax and monetary adjustments which had already been made, together with voluntary restraints and a further turn of the monetary screw, would see us through.

Let me examine first the latter position, as it was perceived in the first half of 1966. The most basic cause for optimism lay in the mighty productive performance and potential, as well as the adaptability, of the American economy. Granted, a Vietnam-charged economy had a voracious appetite for goods and services. But it also had a lot to feed on: (1) an expected increase of 1.8 million persons in civilian employment during 1966 — drawing not only on the normal annual growth of over 1½ percent of the labor force but on the extra growth generated by high employment opportunities, plus a further drop in the unemployment rate; (2) an expansion of perhaps 7 percent in manufacturing capacity during 1966, as the great surge of new plants and equipment continued to come "on stream"; (3) a continuing advance in labor productivity flowing from better tools, training, and technology.

The force of these factors quickly became evident. Industrial production, even after a 40 percent increase in 4½ years of expansion, spurted another 6 percent in the six months after September 1965, when the force of new Vietnam demands hit the economy. Year-end forecasts had to be revised repeatedly, partly to build in greater price increases but also, in significant part, to revise upward the production assumptions. In projecting the real growth of GNP for 1966, private forecasts had generally clustered around a 4½ percent growth assumption; the CEA's forecast was a shade under 5 percent; mine was at 5.2 percent. But within three or four months the economy had shamed us all by moving ahead at a pace that seemed to promise a 5½ percent real-growth rate for the year.[21]

The economic policy doves could cite a number of other impressive factors supporting their position. First, unit-labor costs were behaving surprisingly well under the impact of growing productivity, rapid expansion of the labor force, and the wage-price guideposts. Second, unless Vietnam were to escalate still further, its greatest economic thrust would probably be felt early in 1966 as the immediate impetus of rapidly rising military purchases was reinforced by the advance impulse of a great flow of orders for future delivery. Third, the major braking effect of the new tax bill, tighter money, and $6 billion of new payroll taxes that had gone into effect January 1 was still to come. Fourth, much of the 4-percent rise in wholesale prices in the preceding year had been in food — indeed, producer-finished goods had risen only 1.3 percent in price. Also, as the months wore on, the advance in over-all prices (though not in industrial prices) seemed to abate.

Finally, those who cautioned against further fiscal restraint had on their side the economic skills and persuasive power of President Johnson, whom observers had labeled a "major economic force" and an "economic variable that every forecaster must program into his computations." [22]

He took charge as field commander, drawing on just about every weapon except the nuclear artillery of a tax increase. Every opportunity was used to ease tight supply situations by such measures as releasing metals from government stockpiles, special Department of Labor efforts to ease labor bottlenecks, export quotas on copper and hides, and suspension of import restrictions on lead, zinc, and residual oil. Voluntary restraint efforts were stepped up. Businessmen and bankers were asked to cut back not only their overseas loans and investments but their domestic plant and equipment investments. Appeals to both management and labor to hold wages and prices within guidepost levels were multiplied. Most of these appeals were made behind the scenes. But even the tip of the iceberg that showed — such as the aluminum and copper price rollbacks, the modest steel settlement, and the strict limitation of government pay increases to 3.2 percent — was impressive.

Clearly these efforts represented a new — even if incomplete — chapter in the management of high-pressure prosperity. Thus, one could say, only half in jest, that the economy would not have a recession while Lyndon Johnson was in office — it wouldn't dare! But one hesitated to say the same thing of inflation. Economic history suggested a certain asymmetry here; if the pressures of demand continued to mount, they might sweep before them even the ingenious defenses against inflation erected by the Johnson Administration.

The policy hawks who viewed these demand pressures as excessive and called for new fiscal measures to cut them back also developed impressive support for their case:

First, projections of aggregate consumer, investment, and government demand pointed to quarterly advances averaging about $14 to $15 billion during 1966 against the $11 billion or so that the economy could supply with the kind of price stability we had experienced in 1960–1965. This implied not only price increases, but very tight labor markets and intensified upward pressure on wage rates.

Second, dangers of the contagion of a price-wage spiral, which were minimized in 1966 by a slim calendar of major wage negotiations, would be intensified in 1967 when the calendar would again be full. Some three million workers would be covered by major contracts opening up in 1967 — many of nationwide significance — against less than two million in 1966. An atmosphere of 3-percent advances in consumer prices, coupled with sparkling advances in profits, would be an open invitation to excessive wage increases and rising unit-labor costs.

Third, booming internal demand and rising prices were adversely affecting our competitive position in world markets, encouraging imports and discouraging exports. At a time when our solid progress toward ending the balance-of-payments deficit had already been rudely interrupted by the direct drain of Vietnam, this weakening of our trade balance would further complicate our payments problem.

Fourth, the overexuberant plant and equipment boom was a double source of concern. On the one hand, it was creating inflationary pressures in the machinery, equipment, and construction areas, pressures that could not only fan out to other parts of the economy but worsen our competitive position in a critical area of exports. On the other, although the 7 to 8 percent addition in manufacturing capacity during 1966 might be welcome muscle for Vietnam purposes, it would threaten us with future excess capacity. Under conditions of normal peacetime growth, the U.S. economy absorbs capacity increases of only 4 to 5 percent a year. So the investment boom, if uncurbed, would heighten the risk of a more severe post-Vietnam jolt.

Fifth, the fiscal hawks argued that in the absence of tax action, we would have to rely excessively on tight money. This was objectionable because of its uneven incidence, bearing particularly hard on housing, small business, and state-local government. Also, tight money would put severe pressure on savings institutions. And there were fears of a "ratchet effect" in interest rates. With the increasing impact of U.S. interest rates on those abroad, our rising rates might act as a magnet pulling European rates upward. Then, if our European partners did not play "follow-the-leader" on the way down, we might find that we could not lower our interest rates rapidly in the post-Vietnam period because high, sticky overseas rates would threaten to siphon funds out of this couuntry.

RESOLVING THE POLICY DILEMMA

Reviewing the course of the economic policy debate in the first half of 1966, one is struck by its generally high level. There was no lack of informed and responsible public discussion. There was no lack of economic understanding in high places. There was no lack of public conditioning to a possible tax increase — indeed, there is evidence that a substantial majority of the people expected a tax increase.[23]

But the situation was plagued with uncertainties as to the demands of the war in Vietnam, the economic responses of consumers and business, and the resiliency of the economy in dealing with these pressures. So, even had the President been able to live by economics alone — which, of course, he can never do — he would not have had an open and shut answer: among his official and unofficial advisers on economic matters, the ranks of the "do-it-now" hawks were infiltrated by a substantial number of "wait-and-see" doves.

And beyond economics lay politics. In the Korean situation of 1950 and 1951 Congress had taken the bit in its teeth and enacted three tax increases; but in 1966 the President apparently faced an imposing barrier of congressional reluctance. Part of this was the natural distaste for tax increases, but part of it was an unwillingness to loose the flood of debate on Vietnam for which a tax increase proposal would provide the tempting occasion.

My own view was that the balance of calculated risks called for further action. In the absence of any standby powers permitting "instant taxes" — swift executive moves to put temporary income tax surcharges into effect — I felt that the Administration and the Congress should hammer out a contingency plan for quick activation by joint resolution if the pressures later in 1966 were such as to require it. An alternative would have been to take the contingency label off and simply start a tax bill through Congress with the understanding that a turn for the better in Vietnam and in the economy could halt the process in midstream.

It is easy to say that such proposals are impractical, that

Congress has enough trouble without legislating "as if" tax increases which may never be activated, yet are almost sure to cast some political shadows. Or, as one tax authority in Congress is said to have put it, "Around here you play your cards when you find out what the game is." Yet without standby powers or contingency legislation, the forces of inertia gain unwarranted strength. In 1966 the prospect of several months' time lapse from executive decision to legislative results — a period during which economic winds might have shifted — was itself a barrier to action.

As already implied, the type of tax increase that seemed economically most suitable was a temporary surcharge — perhaps 5 percent — on the corporate and individual income taxes, combined with temporary suspension of the 7-percent investment credit. This program would have netted about $5 billion a year in additional revenues.

My preference for tax increases over expenditure cutbacks (beyond the pruning President Johnson had already done) was based on reasoning which seemed to me conclusive:

First, when the "new economics" called for overt fiscal stimulus in 1961–1965, our chief reliance was on tax reduction — to the tune of nearly $20 billion at 1966 levels of GNP — rather than on increases in Federal civilian expenditures. If we were now to cut the Great Society programs to relieve inflationary pressure, civilian expenditures would, in effect, be the victim both ways.

Second, Federal expenditures on an administrative budget basis had already dropped from 17 percent of GNP in 1955 to 15 percent in 1965–66. Two percentage points may not sound very large, but 2 percent of a $700 billion GNP means that the administrative budget, in relative terms, was $14 billion below its level ten years earlier.[24]

Third, the principles of efficient resource allocation and management call for the development of government programs to accord with basic citizen preferences as between the public and private sectors, rather than their use as stop-and-go instruments of stabilization policy.

Fourth, tax changes have certain operational advantages over expenditure changes for short-run stabilization purposes (not to be confused with long-term expansionary policy). Taxes, once enacted, can go into effect almost immediately through the withholding and current payment system. Further they are much more quickly reversible. A temporary, highly visible surtax could be — and, I believe, would be — removed very quickly to act as an economic stimulant after Vietnam. Beyond this, taxes can be pointed more sharply at the areas' of excess pressure in the economy, for example, at the investment sector.

Finally, in the realm of values, a cutback in Great Society programs would, in effect, finance the war in Vietnam and the fight against inflation largely at the expense of the poor. It seemed far better to cut back private business and consumer spending through the progressive income tax than to slow down our efforts to root out poverty, strengthen education, combat air and water pollution, and restore the rotting core of our cities.

It is too early to bring in the final verdict on the economics of the decision against a further tax increase in the first half of 1966. The web of economic interaction and social values is so tangled that a unanimous, or even a decisive, verdict is probably beyond reach. With politics added in, the verdict is even more difficult. Having viewed at close hand the Presidential dilemma in Kennedy's summer of fiscal discontent in 1962, when the economy plainly needed a tax cut but political reality barred the way, I am not disposed toward a harsh judgment on the 1966 decision. I count on our growing economic maturity to keep on lowering the political barriers to sound economic decisions.

But speaking solely as an economist, and with the benefit of hindsight, I come to this judgment on the tax issue: a temporary tax increase early in 1966, with special focus on the investment sector, would have cost us little in employment opportunities and gained a lot in (a) reducing the pressure of demand inflation in 1966 and of the echoing wage, cost, and price increases in 1967; (b) easing the adverse pressures of the boom on both imports and exports; (c) relieving the undue burdens on monetary policy; and (d) giving us a handy tool — in the form of tax surcharges removed and investment credits restored — to offset the post-Vietnam slack in the economy.

By the summer of 1966, many observers concluded that we had passed the political point of no return on a 1966 tax increase in view of (1) the Congressional elections looming in November, and (2) the temporary easing of economic pressures in the second quarter, when GNP advanced only $11 billion after a $17-billion jump in the first quarter. Focus began to shift to the year-end period when the January budget proposals would be formulated. Even full-time economic policy, it seemed, had its fiscal discontinuities.

The lack of pushbutton procedures or Presidential authority for temporary tax increases was keenly felt.

But inaction was not a foregone conclusion. Relentlessly rising costs of Vietnam, plus a free-spending Congress, brought new pressures to bear on both the budget and the economy. And if these pressures made fiscal action a clear and present necessity, fiscal invention could take any of several forms, for example: appropriated funds for low-priority purposes could be impounded; swift action could be taken to suspend the investment credit or raise taxes on corporate profits; a plan for temporary personal income tax increases could be announced; Congress could come back later in the year via either a pre-election recess or a post-election special session; the House Ways and Means Committee could be convened early to clear the track for quick tax action in January. This illustrative list is meant only to suggest that when an urgent cause creates the will to act, political ingenuity and courage can find a way.

As long as Vietnam escalates, economic policy's primary job will be to cope with demand and cost inflation. And even after the war in Vietnam mercifully abates or ends, there will be the problem of economic "afterglow." For then we may face somewhat the same dilemma as we did after 1957 (though not of the same intensity)—sagging demand, side by side with a delayed round of price and cost increases.

To be realistic, we should expect a post-Vietnam interlude of difficult and delicate economic decisions. Policies may be required to expand demand, production, and jobs. Yet they may be inhibited by price-crawl, cost-push, and

balance-of-payments difficulties which are largely a legacy
of Vietnam pressures that will play themselves out in due
course. We will need to be on guard against the policy trap
of the late 1950's when the battle against inflation was
pressed at heavy cost in income, employment, and growth
even after the enemy had been bested. Unconditional sur-
render was dearly bought.

IMPROVING POLICY TIMING AND STRUCTURE

As a nation we have, I believe, learned the great aggrega-
tive lessons of modern economic policy, even if we have
been hesitant to apply them fully in 1966. We will not
realize their full promise until we also learn, and apply,
the lessons of timing and structure, particularly those
that relate to our fiscal actions. The 1966 experience has
made it plain that if we are to meet the demands of a high-
tension economy with slack in its future, we will need to
push both our thinking and our policy tools in the direction
of greater flexibility, speed, and selectivity, and closer linkage of present and future.

Flexibility and speed. Flexibility of mind, approach, and
program are vital to the success of the "new economics"
in a world of change and uncertainty. This requires willingness to shift or reverse gears, both in the basic direction of
policy and in its emphasis. Again the shifting role of investment serves as a useful example. Just as private capital
spending for modernization and growth was an appropriate
object of our fiscal affection in 1961–1965 when demand
was slack, it became an appropriate object of our temporary
disaffection in 1966 when demand was excessive — when

investment had ballooned to levels at which its longer-term help in cutting costs and generating growth was more than offset by its short-term mischief in intensifying demand pressures and inflationary forces.

Flexibility of program calls for a readiness to move taxes and interest rates up as inflation pressures mount and down as demand ebbs. It calls for shifts between monetary and fiscal, general and selective, measures in response to changes in the structure of our economic problem. And it calls for speed.

The interlocking requirements of flexibility and speed often point to monetary policy as the first line of defense. Habits of mind, ready-made procedures, limited choices, and fairly general agreement on the form of action once its direction is determined, all give monetary policy a decided edge over fiscal policy in speed of action. To narrow the gap calls for further change in our fiscal thinking and practice, especially in taxation.

As to *habits of mind*, we need to get to the point where tax cuts one year to remove slack will not bar temporary tax boosts the next to remove unexpected tension created, for example, by a Vietnam. Selected excise tax reversals in 1966 were a good beginning, but no more than that.

To put *limits on fiscal choices and get advance agreement on form*, President Johnson called for "background studies by both the Congress and Executive Branch . . . to permit quick decisions and prompt action to accommodate short-run cyclical changes." As he said, "If quick action is ever needed, we should not have to begin a long debate on what the changes in taxes should be." [25] A tax package put on the shelf for future use must, of course, balance the interests of speed against those of adaptability to changing circumstances. An advance formula for income tax changes, for example, should provide for some leeway as between individual and corporate income tax changes to permit adjustment to the varying intensity of demand in the investment and consumer sectors.

Most important, we need to develop *streamlined procedures* that can deliver tax changes in a hurry. We need to press the search for shortcuts that are consistent with the congressional prerogative in revenue matters. President Kennedy in 1962 asked for standby Presidential authority, subject to congressional veto, to make quick temporary cuts — up to 5 percentage points — in the individual income tax to fight recession. His request was coldly received by a Congress jealous of its fiscal powers. President Johnson's far milder proposal in 1965 urging Congress to insure "that its procedures will permit rapid action on temporary income tax cuts if recession threatens," did not elicit much response from a Congress otherwise occupied.[26] Although both Presidents focused on recession and tax cuts, the demands of symmetry and realism, as underscored by the 1966 experience, suggest a two-way stretch for speedy fiscal measures to reduce economic instability. In a dynamic economy we cannot assume that the unexpected appearance of either temporary slack and unemployment or bottlenecks and price pressures is a thing of the past.

Perhaps Presidential deadlines can meet the need for speed. The speedy excise tax cuts in 1965 and the quick enactment of the 1966 tax package were impressive cases in point. But recession and inflation wait for no man. We should make every effort to shorten the period between fiscal decision and fiscal action, either by carefully hedged standby powers for the President or by streamlined congressional procedures, or by some combination of the two. If ways and means can be found to cut months to weeks, or weeks to days, in the congressional taxing process in economic emergencies, the cause of stable growth will be well served.

High-speed income tax legislation, quickly translated into changes in withholding and quarterly payment rates, would give the Federal Reserve Board a run for its money in timely stabilization policy. Changes in tax rates still would not be made quite as quickly as changes in discount rates or reserve targets. But with the direct and swift effects of tax rates on the income stream, compared with the slower workings of monetary changes through interest rates and asset changes, fiscal policy would have a fast-cutting edge.

Selectivity. Under this heading, let me make — and illustrate — just two points. First, the differing selective effects of general measures should be given full weight in making decisions on the use of such measures. Second, selective measures like investment credits and installment credit curbs can be useful instruments of stabilization policy. The 1966 investment boom provides illustrations on both counts. It called for measures that could selectively discourage current investment projects and postpone them to the post-Vietnam period. For this dual purpose the expected impact of tighter money on capital spending was as a whole not unwelcome. And temporary suspension of the tax credit for investment — with an ironclad guarantee to restore it — would have served the dual stabilization interest in investments that were "gone today and here tomorrow."

Linking the present and future. As just implied, the ideal policy to use in a high-pressure economy is one that transfers demand to a later, lower-pressure economy. Measures that reduce the return on current capital outlays, with a firm promise to increase the return on future outlays, are especially attractive. Also, anti-inflationary income tax increases that are strictly temporary and quickly reversible can provide a ready source of demand when inflation turns into slack. Making an income tax increase refundable, though not a resounding success in Canada and Great Britain in World War II, also deserves consideration in an economic situation like that created by Vietnam. Knowing that the tax increase is a forced loan rather than a pure tax may somewhat reduce its current impact on private spending, but it will reinforce the commitment to use it in buoying the economy when demand pressures ebb.

Canada's fiscal actions in 1966, under economic circumstances very similar to ours, provide strikingly apt illustrations of the points I have just made. To curb consumer spending, a 1965 individual income tax cut of some 10 percent was largely wiped out in 1966. To provide a powerful dual incentive to defer capital expenditures, special tax exemptions for new investment projects were temporarily suspended, and Canada's 11-percent sales tax on machinery and equipment was cut to 6 percent as of April 1967, and to zero as of April 1968. These pressures to postpone plant and equipment outlays were reinforced by a refundable tax of 5 percent on corporate cash flow, that is, on profits plus depreciation and depletion allowances.

The Canadian parliamentary system permits such tax changes to go into effect the moment the Prime Minister announces them. It is not hard to comprehend why the Canadian tax program in 1966 made the U.S. political economist's mouth water, for here were flexibility, speed, selectivity, and ingenious links between present and future.

POLICY AND PROMISE FOR THE FUTURE

To keep our economic perspective, we need to look beyond the temporary period of economic turbulence during and after Vietnam. Given the experience of the sixties and the advances yet to come, we can confidently count on economic expansion a much higher proportion of the time in the future than in the past. We will have far fewer ups and downs than we did in the 1949–1960 period when we had four recessions. This is not to say that we are about to enter a new era of perpetual prosperity. The "new economics" provides no money-back guarantee against occasional slowdowns or even recessions. As President Johnson has put it, "In principle, public measures can head off recessions before they start. Unforeseen events and mistakes of public or private policy will nonetheless occur. Recessions may be upon us before we recognize their warning signs." [27]

Yet we have good reason to expect the U.S. economy to advance more steadily and, on the average, more rapidly than either its long-run real growth rate of about 3 percent or its postwar rate of 3½ to 4 percent. Growth in real GNP potential should average between 4 and 4½ percent in the coming decade. And with reasonably good management of our prosperity actual growth should not fall much below the growth in potential.

The core of such management will be the skilled deployment of the $7 to $8 billion a year of added Federal revenues automatically generated by normal economic growth. An average advance in GNP of just over 4 percent in real terms, and between 5½ and 6 percent in current prices, will add about $9 billion to the flow of Federal cash receipts each year at existing tax rates. Of this amount, between $1½ and $2 billion will be absorbed by the automatic annual growth in social security benefit payments. This will leave something over $7 billion of new revenue each year — a rise of nearly $40 billion between 1966 and 1971 — to rear its ugly head as fiscal drag or, properly managed, its lovely head in the form of recurring fiscal dividends.

Except in times of excess demand, as already noted, dividends must be declared to be realized. If allowed to turn into fiscal drag they will disappear in economic slack and retarded growth. The choices among alternative forms of dividends may not be easy. Yet they are essentially pleasant choices aimed not at the lesser evil but at the greater good. For they enable us to finance vital new or expanded Federal programs, including a helping hand to the social security system; to provide well-timed tax cuts; and to make more generous transfers of funds to hard-pressed state and local governments. Just to list these choices is to make clear that although they are in part economic — because some combi-

nations will deliver more growth and stability than others
— the proper mix will depend even more on the country's
social and political priorities.

The demands of Vietnam and of anti-inflationary policy,
together with the inescapable growth in certain civilian expenditures, may preempt the dividends for the immediate
future. On the other hand, it is quite possible that the need
and opportunity to declare such dividends may reappear
sooner than we think.

The remarkable power of our Federal revenue system is
such that, if defense spending were to level off at the rate
programmed in the fiscal 1967 budget (which, alas, it
won't), a potential fiscal drag of some $12 billion would
develop by fiscal 1969, and would reach nearly $20 billion
by fiscal 1970 (before allowing for increases in nondefense
spending other than programmed increases in personal
transfers and interest payments). We would still be fighting
a war overseas, and yet have to take deliberately expansionary fiscal steps to maintain the health of our economy at
home. If we did not, having shown that we can have both
guns and butter in 1966, we could find ourselves risking
both war and recession in 1968. Our great strength is that
our economy is capable of so much. Our weakness would
be a failure to make full use of this capability.

The size of the immediate fiscal feast once Vietnam ends
will depend in part on our budgetary target at high employment. If money rates come down readily and private
investment demand is strong, first claim on our rising
revenues would be to hold some of them as a high-employment surplus for debt retirement. But if money rates prove

to be stubborn, or if business investment and housing demands — with or without easy money — do not rise to the occasion, a balanced budget at high employment might again be the appropriate target.

Given this target, and leaving aside the extra post-Vietnam dividends, we need to refer to past experience to see how much of the $7 billion-plus a year might be claimed by "normal" growth in Federal civilian expenditures. These expenditures — which are net of defense and space spending and the trust fund outlays already allowed for — rose by an average of less than $2½ billion annually between the fiscal years 1955 and 1966. This pace suggests that we will have ample leeway not only to step up the tempo of our Great Society programs but to share some of the revenue bounty with Federal taxpayers and state-local treasuries. How should these prospective fiscal dividends be apportioned among the competing claimants to realize the full promise of modern economic policy?

THE SOURCES AND USES OF GROWTH

If the U.S. economy of the future will be, not recession-proof, but at least recession-repellent — as I believe it will — we can and should focus more and more of our future economic policy attention on growth, on its sources, its costs, and its uses.

I am not unmindful that the economic growth we measure is not everything. There is more to economic life than goods and services, and more to life than economic life. Justice, freedom, valor, leisure, and wit are not counted in the national product — not because they are unimportant parts of the good life, but because they cannot be measured — the markets for justice and valor are too thin to yield reliable price quotations.

Also I am keenly aware that Galbraith's "penultimate western man, stalled in the ultimate traffic jam and slowly succumbing to carbon monoxide," will hardly be enchanted "to hear from the last survivor that in the preceding year Gross National Product went up by a record amount." [28]

The picture of a mindless and heartless process of growth that Galbraith puts before us is, I am sure, part of an effort to get us to put our minds and hearts to redirecting its fruits toward uses of high purpose and quality. This is all well and good. I would only add that unless we first put our backs to it we will have no fruits to redirect.

So future fiscal dividends must be declared with an eye not just to the uses but to the *sources* of growth. In the past few years part of our rise to the top of the growth ladder has been accomplished by closing the GNP, or production, gap. With the economy operating at or near its potential, our realized growth in the future will depend chiefly on the rate of increase in that potential. We can no longer pad the figure, so to speak, by taking up economic slack.

Rising productivity will be the key. In part, this will require continued measures to maintain high levels of private investment in plant and equipment. In part, also, it calls for measures to improve efficiency and hence productivity by adjustments — many of them politically painful — in our policies for transportation, manpower allocation, agriculture, and the like. Advances on these microeconomic fronts are long overdue.

But beyond this — and especially if balance-of-payments considerations bar the use of easy money as a growth stimulant, or if further fiscal and monetary encouragements were to add but little to the sustainable rate of private investment — the search for faster growth of our productive capacity will lead us ever more directly to wellsprings that only government can provide through its investment in education, research, and physical resources. When we add to this the Federal government's responsibility for overcoming some of the *ravages* of economic growth, and its commitment to those *uses* of growth that will raise the quality of life, Federal expenditures become a top claimant on the fiscal dividends in our future.

THE ROLE OF FEDERAL EXPENDITURES

Public expenditure programs will play a large part in pushing out the social and scientific frontiers that will define our economy's limits in the future. They will enter into the economic growth equation in critically important ways.

Programs to develop human resources will pay enormous rewards in higher productivity. One of the significant contributions of empirical work in economics in recent years is the better measurement and increased understanding of education and work skills as a source of more rapid growth. Further expansion of our manpower programs — especially now that we are in a range where structural unemployment *does* become important — promises good returns in expanding the economy's potential. The National Commission on Technology, Automation, and Economic Progress, in its 1966 report, urged expansion of Federal retraining efforts after describing the program to date as still "experimental in scale." [29]

For the longer run the big payoff will come from basic education. It is no coincidence that the over-all superiority of the American school system is matched by the higher productivity of American workers. Yet we remain far below what is achievable in educating our children. The Automation Commission strongly underscored this point and recommended that free education be extended from the standard 12 to 14 years, with technical schools and community colleges playing a major role.[30]

Another intangible but significant contribution by government to the growth process is through its large outlays on research. The resulting advances in technology raise the quality and efficiency of both private and public capital.

Enlarging the stock of tangible public capital has also long been recognized as a government responsibility in the growth process. Public roads, water systems, school buildings and hospitals will be no less important in the future because they are already on the familiar lists of the past. Direct government investment in atomic energy, in communication satellites, in mass transportation, and in urban redevelopment are less traditional but equally important.

New programs of public support of research, public construction, and public operation are looming larger in the quest for future supplies of natural resources. Water resources alone are the subject of desalinization experiments, pollution control, weather modification — all part of a list of exciting and important areas in which the public return may prove to be as large in the future as the returns in agricultural research, for example, have been in the past.

While seeking to expand our efficiency and gain the benefits of faster growth, we cannot weigh the future claims of growth on public expenditures by this criterion alone. At bottom, growth is to be enjoyed — and, most importantly, in a good society, it is to be enjoyed by all.

First claim on the *products* of growth should be to repair the ravages of the growth *process*. If as *byproducts* in our quest for growth, we destroy the purity of our air and water, generate ugliness and social disorder, displace workers and their skills, gobble up our natural resources, and chew up the amenities in and around our cities, the repair of that damage should have first call on the proceeds of growth. If the damage is essentially a private cost forced on society, as in the case of industrial effluents and smoke discharge, it should be forced back on those private units. But much of the problem and the cost can be met only by government. (If we could isolate that part of it which is a direct cost or byproduct of growth from that which is a natural concomitant of population growth and urbanization and so forth, we should probably make a subtraction each year from our total output, an adjustment of our GNP figures, to take account of it.)

When we turn to the *uses* of growth, we find a rather blurred line between programs to speed its advance and overcome its costs, on one hand, and programs to devote its product to the better life, on the other. Each of us has his own conception of these uses. I have put mine this way:

The polluted air I breathe in many large cities, the now polluted Lake Michigan, Milwaukee River, and Puget Sound waters I used to swim in as a boy, our vanishing wilderness, our growing urban blight, the persistence of human poverty amidst plenty, the uneven struggle between beauty and ugliness in our surroundings, the excessive incidence of illiteracy, crime, and delinquency — all these reach out for a large share of that $7 billion annual dividend, either in the form of direct programs or through more generous transfers to state and local governments. For how else are we to gain control of our public environment, rather than letting it control us in a "half-finished society" . . . ? How else can we make real progress toward a society that will not only be large and productive but great and good? [31]

TAX CUTS

One need not dwell on the claim of the tax-cutters of the future. They will point out, correctly, that tax cuts vitalize free markets and private incentives, supply added funds for private capital formation, and boost private demand. Yet I would hope that the tax cut lesson of the past few years has been learned wisely, but not *too* well. The on-target success of the 1964 tax cut should not blind us to the special circumstances that made massive tax cuts the clear choice over more rapid expenditure increases at that time — circumstances that may not repeat themselves in the near future.

First, the income-tax rate structure itself badly needed realignment, particularly in the top and bottom brackets. This meant lowering the top-bracket rates to reduce avoidance and restore incentives and the low-bracket rates to meet the elementary requirements of equity.

Second, there was a companion need to halt and reverse

the process of erosion of the income tax base in the interests of both greater equity and less distortion of resource allocation. The large tax cut was a promising vehicle for this purpose, even though it was finally accompanied by only modest reforms.

Third, the pressing need for private investment in modernization of the nation's plant and equipment pointed to expansion of aggregate demand by methods that would increase incentives for risk-taking and enlarge the flow of investment funds.

Fourth, the whole political complex in its broadest sense required an approach to expansionary policy which would not be rejected on grounds that it necessarily meant bloated budgets. Added expenditure programs faced very great resistance. The use of tax reduction made it possible to induce a coalition of conservative and liberal forces to endorse and work for an expansionary fiscal policy even in the face of an existing deficit, an expanding economy, and rising government expenditures.

Fifth, under the foregoing circumstances, the surest path to more adequately financed government programs was, paradoxically, through tax reduction. The upsurge of tax revenues flowing from economic expansion would finance higher levels of local, state, and Federal spending than we would have had without the tax cut's stimulus — a stimulus that the country was unwilling to provide by deliberately enlarging the Federal budget. President Kennedy's persuasion on this point was reflected in a comment he made to me just eleven days before his death, "First we'll get your tax cut, and then we'll get my expenditure programs." And, in point of fact, the 16.9 percent rise in GNP in the two years after the tax cut — between the first quarters of 1964 and 1966 — made possible a 13.5 percent rise in government expenditures at lower average tax rates.

The case for Federal tax cuts as the chosen weapon to remove fiscal drag will be a good deal less compelling in the future than it was in 1963–1965. Better public understanding of the "new economics" will open up other options. Some of the most glaring defects in the income-tax rate structure have been corrected. The excise tax structure has been purged. A much better tax climate for investment has been created. And both Federal programs and state-local governments will be pressing strong and valid claims to a bigger cut of the fiscal melon. Yet the rise in Federal revenues will be so great that some income tax cuts, both individual and corporate, will be possible and desirable as part of the over-all pattern of fiscal dividends for — and from — economic growth.

Something of a consensus seems to be developing, as it should, that top priority in longer-term tax reduction belongs to the low-income groups. The gradual price creep, rising productivity, higher living standards, and mounting payroll and state-local consumption taxes have all combined to make our personal exemption levels obsolete. So I fully agree with former Secretary of the Treasury Douglas Dillon that, in addition to the 1964 action on minimum standard deductions and splitting of the first bracket, "both interests of tax fairness, as well as the need to lighten the burden of true poverty, call for further action." [32] President Johnson made this position official when he said, in signing the excise tax bill in 1965, "We hope, in particular, to provide further tax relief to those in our Nation who need it most — those taxpayers who now live in the shadow of poverty." [33]

Proposals for payment of a negative income tax or provision of a guaranteed income — through a universal social dividend or "demogrant" — are more far-reaching steps in the same direction. It is a reflection both of our economic growth and of our increasing social maturity that such programs now gain the benefit of calm and rational discussion, together with gradually increasing support, in contrast with the emotional and hostile reaction they touched off not so many years ago.

We are, of course, far from a majority in favor of such proposals. For example, a Minnesota Poll early in 1966 found only 24 percent of the respondents saying "yes" when they were asked whether "people who live in poverty should be paid what is called a negative income tax." [34] But since I can recall the grumbling and murmurs about "teaching communism of income" when I used the negative income tax as a teaching device at the University of Minnesota some twenty years ago (when it was first discussed among fiscal economists), I am inclined to view a roughly one-fourth favorable vote as considerable progress.

Closely allied to special forms of income tax reduction to aid the lowest income groups is the proposal to finance increases in social security benefits, both scheduled and unscheduled, out of general revenues. How far should we go in further across-the-board income tax cuts side by side with payroll tax increases that bear most heavily on the lower income groups, bear heavily on consumption, and increase employers' costs of providing jobs? As fiscal leeway develops, I believe we can make a strong case for strengthening our system of income maintenance without corresponding increases in payroll taxes. As a first step, one might well tap the income tax to finance higher unemployment compensation payments. It would strengthen the economy and ease burdens on small incomes without raising business costs.

A parallel question arises from the state-local side: how much further should we go in cutting Federal income taxes while we steadily boost our generally regressive state-local property, sales and excise taxes? Just in case the question does not answer itself, I will take it up in Chapter III.

The promise of modern economic policy, managed with an eye to maintaining prosperity, subduing inflation, and raising the quality of life, is indeed great. And although we have made no startling conceptual breakthroughs in economics in recent years, we *have*, more effectively than ever before, harnessed the existing economics — the economics that has been taught in the nation's college classrooms for some twenty years — to the purposes of prosperity, stability, and growth. As we have seen, we cannot relax our efforts to increase the technical efficiency of economic policy. But it is also clear that its promise will not be fulfilled unless we couple with improved techniques of economic management a determination to convert good economics and a great prosperity into a good life and a great society.

§ CHAPTER III § Strengthening the Fiscal Base of Our Federalism

Just as Federal economic policy making and policy itself have taken on new dimensions, the fiscal problems of federalism are entering a new stage. After years of wandering in the wilderness of "political problems which are insoluble and economic problems which are incomprehensible" — to adapt a favorite phrase of Sir Alec Douglas-Home — Federal-state-local fiscal relations are at last on the threshold of a promised land created by vigorous economic growth and balanced political reapportionment. Growth is generating a flow of Federal revenues which will permit the study of major new fiscal coordination devices to move from the barren ground of hypothetical discussion — where it has languished for thirty or forty years — to the fertile ground of practical, fundable proposals. And reapportionment will strengthen the legislative base for new initiatives to revitalize the states.

In looking anew at methods to strengthen the fiscal base of our federalism, we are dealing with a combination of economic and political forces which provides ideal grist for the mill of applied political economy. So the scholar who is happiest in the austere Never-Never-Land of logical positivism will find cold comfort in this chapter. But the man of affairs who yearns for the value-laden Ever-Ever-Land of normative choices will find himself very much at home.

The great prosperity that opens these new fiscal vistas presents the two faces of Janus to different levels of government. At the Federal level, economic growth and a powerful tax system, interacting under modern fiscal management, generate new revenues faster than they generate new demands on the Federal purse. But at the state-local level, the situation is reversed. Under the whiplash of prosperity, responsibilities are outstripping revenues. As Galbraith has suggested, prosperity gives the Federal government the revenues, and the state and local governments the problems. Or as L. L. Ecker-Racz has said: "There is no escaping the conflict because . . . national progress bestows both bounties and burdens: the bounties tend to be national, the burdens State and local." [1] Nevertheless, the dominant note, and the hopeful one, is that the Federal revenue flow is now large enough to redress the fiscal balance under peacetime conditions.

Side by side with this new economic-fiscal dimension is the new political-constitutional dimension of the Supreme Court's reapportionment decisions. It is redressing the political balance in state legislatures away from rotten boroughs and lopsided rural representation toward the urban, and especially the suburban, constituencies. This offers us the prospect of new blood, greater responsiveness, and greater vitality in our state legislatures. This promise was painted in glowing terms by Senator Joseph D. Tydings recently when he said that "the Supreme Court's reapportionment decisions, which the self-proclaimed champions of 'states' rights' so bitterly assail, will do more to rebuild our withering federal system than any other event in this century." [2]

So the promise of reapportionment, the prospect of Federal fiscal dividends, and the fact of severe fiscal pressure on the states all call for a new look at the Federal-state-fiscal relationship. Successes on the new frontiers of positive Federal economic policy enable us to explore some of the old frontiers of our federalism and to take positive steps to strengthen and secure those frontiers.

The way in which we resolve the problem of fiscal imbalance will have a profound effect on the future course and strength of our federalism.

It will have a major impact, first of all, on the harshness of the terms on which state and local governments reconcile their rapidly rising expenditure obligations and their limited — and often overworked — tax base. Balance their budgets, they will — indeed, under most state constitutions, they must. But the key question is — on what terms, both as to the level of public services and as to the regressiveness of their tax structures, will they strike this balance?

Second, the size and form of Federal fiscal support to state-local government will be a major factor in shaping our national fiscal system in the longer run. It will strongly influence both the over-all distribution, by income groups, of our Federal-state-local fiscal burdens and the pattern and extent of geographical inequalities in tax burdens and service levels.

And, third, the way we resolve this question will affect the relative strength of Federal and state-local governments. Or, to put it differently, it will affect the basic role and vitality of the states.

Vietnam, of course, has postponed the happy day when the hopes of the states for some new and generous form of Federal financial support can be realized. First, the requirements of Vietnam itself must be met. Second, putting the Great Society programs back on schedule will demand large sums. Third, occasional talk of a $20 billion antimissile defense system has a chilling contingent impact on state hopes.

But the power of the Federal revenue system is so great, and the pressure of state-local needs so unrelenting, that the basic issue will be ever with us. Given the fiscal, political, and philosophical swamps and thickets through which we have to thread our way en route to a resolution of this financial dilemma, we have no time to lose in putting our minds to it.

THE ROLE OF THE STATES

A determination to strengthen the weak state-local link in our fiscal federalism must be anchored in the conviction that the states are here to stay, that they do play an indispensable role in our federal system of government.

We need to be sure, in other words, that we still believe in a federalism rather than a unitary government — that we would not accept the view of my Parisian friend, a scientist, who wrote recently to applaud what he calls the "phagocytosis" of the states by the Federal initiative, their transformation into "sectors or departments." He said, admiringly, that "from a federation the United States are at last becoming a nation." And I thought, "How French!" Yet it was his countryman, Alexis de Tocqueville, who pointed out, well over a century ago, that although a continental country can be successfully governed centrally, it cannot be successfully administered centrally. Richard Goodwin adds that with regard to the nation's problems today, "We are not wise enough to solve them from the top, nor are there resources enough to solve them from the bottom." [3]

But, more specifically, is there a truly persuasive case — one that we will accept as a cause for action — for revitalizing and strengthening the states as units in our federal structure? I believe there is.

One can put it in terms of the negative imperative of de Tocqueville and Goodwin that there is neither the administrative capacity nor the problem-solving wisdom at the top. Or, to put it more bluntly, the Federal government simply cannot carry out large segments of its responsibilities at all — or at all efficiently — without strengthening the states and localities. A very large part of what we do through government is done through state and local units. They are the ones to whom we usually turn as we seek to maintain and upgrade our educational efforts, improve our physical and mental health, redevelop decaying urban areas, build safer and better highways, overcome air and water pollution, and equip our suburbs with water systems, sewers, roads, parks, schools, and the like. This list is striking partly because each item on it represents either an essential function or a reasonable aspiration of a great and growing society; partly because each item falls squarely within the traditional sphere of state-local operations; and partly because so many items on the list are suffused with a national interest that transcends state and local lines and demands Federal action and support.

Education is a case in point. State and local governments raise about 90 percent and spend 100 percent of the funds we devote to public schooling. Yet education is an essential instrument for carrying out functions that are a direct Federal responsibility. Education is an investment in human brainpower from which we reap positive gains in the form of higher productivity, more rapidly advancing technology, a better informed foreign policy, and a stronger national defense. In this light, one might add, Federal support of locally operated and locally controlled public education is no act of charity or largesse. It is simply creative and cooperative federalism at work, a means of discharging certain national obligations through traditionally local institutions. Local initiative and effort are already harnessed to the national interest. Federal funds simply mean that the national interest in the results will be matched by a national effort in financing them.

One may also observe that each decade, one sixth of the U.S. population changes its residence across state lines. Our great mobility, combined with sharply unequal educational opportunities, again involves the national interest. Inequality plus mobility means that no community is immune to the effects of substandard education. Only the *federation* of states — operating through its agents, namely, the President and the Congress — can surmount this problem. How? By taking over the schools? No, by providing the equalizing financial support needed to raise the national floor of education to at least an acceptable minimum.

If we want state and local governments to be efficient partners in our federalism, we have to strengthen the whole fabric of government at their levels. Great inequality in the access to knowledge, in the available skills, and in the techniques used — in a word, in the competence of government — will distort and endanger the partnership. It will create disparities in the capacity for planning, and for effective action, and thus lead to inefficiency and frustration. The potential for constructive cooperation is undermined when state-local government is so understaffed — both quantitatively and qualitatively — and so underfinanced that it cannot meet the Federal bureaucracy on reasonably even terms.

Getting a bit ahead of our story, I might note that these inequalities have been recognized and dealt with on a function-by-function basis through our myriad Federal grants-in-aid. These have served to reduce disparities and increase the quality of service in many specific areas of state-local activity. But we still seek the fiscal formula that will improve the *total* capability of state-local government, and with it, of government as a whole. States and localities — either as they now exist, or perhaps with growing emphasis on both regional and metropolitan-area groupings — will continue to be the service centers through which important national purposes are achieved. If we don't want those purposes thwarted or diluted, we had better strengthen these operating units.

But that is not the whole story. There are also more positive reasons why the states and their subdivisions should have a stronger role. Creative federalism requires diversity and dissent and innovation. Yet these cannot simply come down from on high. They have to well up from below. The danger if they do not is that the central government will grow stronger in authority and weaker in ideas. Clearly, under President Johnson's concept of creative federalism, state and local governments are not the only sources of creative ground swell. The creative process can also center in the universities, in nonprofit foundations, in poverty-program councils, in hospitals, and so on.[4] But the states and localities are still the most essential part of a mechanism for feeding ideas up the line and having them come back down with money attached.

We tend to think that the innovative fire in the states went out with the elder Robert La Follette. And, in truth, it is not easy to visualize any state of the future matching Wisconsin's path-breaking leadership in income taxes, in unemployment compensation, in public utility regulation, and in public administration — leadership fueled in substantial part by ideas flowing from the University to the State House. But neither is it hard to find contemporary evidence of innovation and pioneering in the states. To illustrate their role as "innovators of enlightened programs of government," Senator Edward M. Kennedy cites Kentucky's highway beautification program, Virginia's Department of Aging, Rhode Island's medicare program, and California's measures to combat air pollution from automobiles.[5] One can add Wisconsin's outdoor recreation program, California's system of two-year community colleges, and North Carolina's poverty program.[6] And perhaps Nevada's open gambling laws and New Hampshire's state lottery deserve inclusion as experiments — quarantined by state boundary lines — which will prove to be fine examples of "how not to do it." Thus, Justice Brandeis' "laboratories of the federal system" have not gone out of business.

Finally, one need not dwell on the virtues of state and local governments as the chosen instruments of the political decentralization and dispersion of power essential to a democracy. Their role here is well known. But that makes it no less fundamental.[7]

My basic premise, then, is that to the simple question, "Do you want stronger state government?" the country's answer is unequivocally, "We do." If we do not accept that basic premise, if we are unrelenting Hamiltonians — or perhaps Spencerians who yearn for that government that governs least, who stand on their states' rights so they can sit on them — then all of the succeeding syllogisms, no matter how logically unassailable, will not convince us that Federal revenues should be shared more generously with the states.

STATE-LOCAL FISCAL PRESSURES

The next point in the fiscal syllogism is also simple: the states just cannot go it alone fiscally. To put it crudely, we have to find some sort of joint fiscal solution to their enormous and growing problems which will enable governors to be bold and innovative and expansionary and wake up the day after election still in office. Again and again, good governors have been defeated by the higher taxes they have had to espouse to finance their innovations and expansion. This was borne in on me most vividly in 1960 when Governor Orville Freeman of Minnesota was running for a fourth two-year term. He made a point of forthrightly telling the voters that "there ain't no Santa Claus," that if they wanted the services, they would have to pay for them in higher taxes. And after the election, he woke up, not governor, but Secretary of Agriculture — where, in the eyes of some critics, he *is* Santa Claus (though he may feel more like Scrooge).

Even apart from the political hazards of raising taxes, the states have to cope with serious economic and institutional handicaps.

First and foremost, interstate competition, and fears of losing industry and wealth, not only inhibit state-local taxing efforts but push them in regressive directions. In speaking of this destructive and self-defeating tax competition, Ecker-Racz notes that although "the influence of tax considerations on the location decisions of business is grossly overstated . . . its impact on state and local taxation is not." I doubt that he overstates the case when he says: "Fear of losing business to another jurisdiction haunts the mind and stills the pen of the state and local lawmaker, and special pleaders have developed the skill of exploiting this fear to a high art." [8]

Second, limited jurisdiction and small size deny local and state tax agencies most of the economies of scale enjoyed by the Internal Revenue Service, hamper their administrative and enforcement efforts, and bias state-local taxing systems toward the property and consumption taxes.

The third handicap arises largely out of the first two. In contrast to Federal reliance on growth-responsive taxes — taxes whose revenue rises proportionately faster than the gross national product — states and localities depend largely on taxes that respond sluggishly. They draw nearly four fifths of their total tax revenues from sources — property taxes (45 percent) and sales and gross-receipts taxes (33 percent) — whose yields, at stable tax rates, barely keep pace with the growth of the economy, rising a trifle less than 10 percent for every 10-percent rise in GNP. They draw only 8 percent from the highly responsive state personal income tax, whose revenues grow 16 to 18 percent for every 10-percent rise in GNP.[9]

Limited state reliance on income taxes reminds us of a fourth barrier, namely, heavy Federal reliance on selected tax sources. References to the Federal preemption of the income tax are not uncommon. Since the Federal government allows the deduction of state income taxes in arriving at taxable income — thus shielding taxpayers, especially those in the higher income groups, from the full impact of duplication — and since the states that are the heaviest users of the personal income tax have effective rates (as a percent of Federal adjusted gross income) eight times as high as those that make lightest use of the tax, one has difficulty distinguishing between reason and excuse.

Nonetheless, it seems clear that the high Federal income tax does inhibit the states and localities in the use of this progressive tax source, for how else would one explain the virtual halt in state income tax enactments in the 1940's and 1950's?

Beleaguered state-local officials see Federal-state fiscal disparities in even bolder relief when they turn their attention from their viscous tax sources to the free-flowing budgetary uses of their revenues. From 1955 to 1965, state-local expenditures rose by 125 percent, nearly twice the Federal increase of 65 percent. Federal spending thus lagged behind the 70 percent growth in GNP during the same period. But state-local spending grew 80 percent faster than GNP.[10] At the end of the period the state-local share in total civilian government spending was 77 percent, the Federal share only 23 percent. Even if we shift Federal grants-in-aid into the Federal expenditure column, the ratio is still two thirds to one third.

What these figures reflect is not a conscious assertion of states' rights and responsibilities, a renewed and conscious pursuit of the virtues of local self-government, but a response to the irresistible pressures of population, prosperity, and price trends.

Population burdens state-local budgets, not just by its 17-percent over-all growth from 1955 to 1965, but by its composition — by the 37-percent rise in the school-age population and the 25-percent rise in the over-65 group. And population is not only growing fast but moving fast, particularly into urban areas. From 1950 to 1960 the population in metropolitan areas increased from 56 to 63 percent of the U.S. population, and by 2000 the figure will be 75 percent. Per capita government expenditures and revenues average some 30 percent higher in metropolitan areas than elsewhere. Mobility and urbanization — and particularly the flight to the suburbs — call for ever *more* schools, roads, parks, sewers, for more and costlier services.

Meanwhile, *prosperity* generates demands for *better* schools, roads, and parks, for new and better services. And it generates them faster than it produces added state-local revenues. Further, the growth that confers such a bountiful harvest of revenues on the Federal government leaves the states and their subdivisions a bitter harvest of air and water pollution, disappearing green space, and urban rot. Truly, prosperity gives the national government the affluence and the local governments the effluents.

Price trends, too, work against state-local budgets. From 1960 to 1965 the increase in the state-local price deflator — a measure of the price increases of goods and services bought by state and local governments — averaged 3 percent a year. This was a bit more than double the increase in the over-all GNP deflator. Going back another five years does not change the picture: from 1955 to 1965 prices paid by state-local governments rose 40 percent — including a 60-percent rise in teachers' salaries — while the GNP price deflator rose roughly 20 percent. Given the present $70 billion a year of state-local purchases, one has to add $2 billion a year simply to take care of price increases.[11]

One can go on in the words of Orville Freeman: "And consider this irony of the inflation situation. If price levels continue to rise, the figures just quoted indicate that our state budgets will suffer proportionately more than family budgets, business budgets, and Federal budgets. At the same time, if the Federal Reserve System puts on the tight money screws in its efforts to stop inflation . . . the interest rates in our tremendous borrowing program rise sharply. What happens? We are caught either way, or perhaps I should say, both ways." His words were written in the summer of 1959.[12]

STATE-LOCAL FISCAL EFFORTS

In meeting these unrelenting pressures, state and local bodies should, can, and will do more to tax themselves. That they have not been standing idly by is amply demonstrated by the recent fiscal record. While an average cut of 15 percent in Federal tax rates since 1961 was bringing the ratio of Federal tax collections to the GNP down to its lowest point since the war — 14.4 percent in 1964 — state tax rates were rising sharply, continuing the trend that has increased the share of state-local taxes in the GNP from 5.4 percent in 1946 to 8.0 percent in 1964.[13]

In the 1955–1965 decade states and localities increased revenues from their own sources from $28 to $63 billion, or by an average of 8.6 percent a year. Meanwhile, Federal grants-in-aid grew from $3 billion to $11 billion. In other words, the states financed from their own sources about 85 cents out of each dollar of new spending. And hard as they have worked their reluctant tax sources since the war, raising their yields more than five-fold, they have raised their net debt even faster — from less than $14 billion in

1946 to roughly $95 billion twenty years later, a seven-fold increase.

The remarkable fiscal efforts made by state-local government are also reflected in the brisk business in new and used taxes that was done by the state legislatures from January 1965 through June 1966. Five states enacted new sales taxes (Idaho, Massachusetts, New Jersey, New York, and Virginia), while eight others increased their rates. A new personal income tax was enacted in Nebraska, and eight other states increased rates. Eight increased their corporate income tax rates. Oregon, long a holdout, adopted a cigarette tax, while fifteen others increased rates. Finally, seven states increased liquor tax rates and ten, gasoline tax rates. This list translates the growing pressures on the states into vivid and painful specifics.

The spate of tax increases attests not only to the great fiscal pressure on state governments but to their fiscal courage, their fiscal effort, and, one might add, their fiscal ingenuity. Starting with Indiana in 1963 — and Colorado, Hawaii, and Massachusetts have followed suit since then — income tax credits are being used to take the regressive curse off sales taxes. In effect, these states build a personal exemption into the sales tax by granting a per capita credit (Indiana's $6 credit amounts to a $300 per capita exemption under its 2-percent sales tax) which can either be deducted from state income tax liabilities, or if none exist, claimed as a cash refund. Massachusetts limits its credit to those whose taxable income does not exceed $5,000. Hawaii has put its credit on a gradually diminishing basis as income increases. These refinements are aimed at converting the sales tax into a progressive tax. Through this inter-locking of sales and income taxes, we may yet make a silk purse out of a sow's ear.[14]

Giving states and localities an A-plus for their tax efforts is not, of course, to say that they have done all they should. Until local government structure is reformed, until state-local tax administration is strengthened, until the laggard states and localities raise their tax efforts to the levels of the leaders, one's praise must be qualified. But to infer that the Federal government should not enlarge its fiscal sup-port of the states until they have taken these steps, as some critics do, not only ignores the Herculean efforts that have been made, but fails to see that greater Federal support and growing state-local reform can go hand in hand, in-deed, that such support can facilitate or even stimulate reform.

THE COMMANDING CASE
FOR FEDERAL SUPPORT

Twenty years of spectacular growth in state-local taxes and Federal grants-in-aid have brought no let-up in the fiscal pressure. Is any respite in sight? Rough projections from past experience, not surprisingly, do not suggest any. Even assuming a slowdown in the growth rate of state-local spending to 7 percent a year (from its 8½ percent pace of the past decade), Joseph Pechman projected state-local general expenditures at $103 billion in 1970. Keeping pace with an assumed GNP growth of 5 percent annually, state-local receipts (including Federal grants) would reach only $88 billion, leaving a $15 billion gap.[15]

A more detailed estimate by Dick Netzer puts general expenditures at $104.5 billion in 1970, 40 percent above the 1964 level. He puts total revenue needs at $121 billion and available receipts at $111 billion. To close this $10 billion gap by added state-local tax collections would require an 18-percent increase in state-local tax rates.[16] Selma Mushkin and Gabrielle Lupo, in their Project '70 study, see much the same total revenue needs ($122 billion), but see no gap under their "high revenue" assumption (which includes $86 billion of general revenues, $22 billion of Federal aid, and $15 billion of gross borrowing), and only a small gap under their "low revenue assumption." [17]

Each of these projections is reasonable, given its assumptions. And the broad assumptions of each are also within reason. Two show sizable gaps to be closed by state-local taxes or other measures, while the third draws on an assumed doubling of Federal grants in five years, together with a rise in gross borrowing, to cover revenue requirements in 1970.

Since the third — the Mushkin-Lupo projection — is the most recent and exhaustive, it will probably lead some observers to conclude that state and local governments can meet future revenue needs without undue strain. But before anyone reaches this complacent conclusion, let him knock on any fiscal door or scratch any fiscal surface at the state or local level — let him probe the reality that lies behind and beneath the statistics he uses as his point of departure.

Let him find a single major city or state that is not under fiscal duress, that can meet its pressing needs and aspirations without fiscal heroics.

Let him look in his own suburb and see the unmet needs for school facilities, sewers, sidewalks, street lights, green space, more frequent garbage and trash collection. Or in his central city, let him observe the rutted streets and crumbling curbs, the deteriorating parks and the miserable housing in the urban ghettos, the massive fight still ahead of us against poverty, delinquency, and crime. Or in his state, let him not be misled by the temporary fiscal frosting of surpluses from the unexpected surge in revenues growing out of the Vietnam-charged boom. There's hardtack, not cake, just underneath: the near-doubling of higher education expenditures in the next five years; the fight against air and water pollution which has only just begun; the crying needs for better prisons and mental hospitals.

Nor should he forget that thousands of school districts in our rural and urban slums need to raise their teachers' salaries to (or, in logic, beyond) the national average of $6,800, and that the average districts aspire to the $10,000 salaries and the kindergarten and preschool programs of the leading districts. Let him contemplate the fiscal plight of New York City or the curious sight of California, one of our richest states, breathlessly trying to catch up with its galloping governmental needs. And let him count the cost of keeping up with pioneering states which, like the Joneses, "keep on doing things we can't afford": for example, New York's billion-dollar program to purify its waters; or its Medicaid program with its startling costs; or Wisconsin's outdoor recreation program; or California's community colleges.

And lest the man of means thinks he can insulate himself from these problems and poisons, let him fly into Los Angeles on a smoggy day, or sail on a polluted river or bay, or hire the products of substandard schooling, or assure his family and business of adequate supplies of pure water. Even with large private means, he cannot "buy free" of all the problems created by the neglect of state-local fiscal health.

Statistical projections, then, are essential for planning, for defining our problems. But projections are not forecasts, and forecasts are not goals. Our fiscal planning for federalism has to prepare for the worst — for the minimum demanded by quantitative projections — while it plans for the best — for the maximum demanded by our qualitative goals and aspirations in a framework of abundance.

But statistical projections alone tend to beg the question. That question, as noted early in our discussion, is not *whether* states and localities can make ends meet, but *on what terms*. On terms that just cover the irresistible minimum or that meet our aspirations? On terms that force our Federal-state-local tax system into a more and more regressive mold or that protect its progressivity? On terms that perpetuate the great inequalities among the states or that steadily reduce them? On terms that will enable state and local governments to become vital and creative cogs in the machine of federalism, or just overburdened service stations? That brings us face to face with the question of what kind of fiscal federalism we want.

Out of the $28-billion increase in state and local tax revenues between 1955 and 1965, 44 percent came from increased property taxes, 34 percent from increased sales and gross receipts taxes, and only 14 percent from individual and corporate income taxes. Coupled with sharp reductions in Federal income tax rates during the same period and increases in social security payroll taxes, the increases in state-local taxes are moving us in a regressive direction. In sketching the national fiscal blueprint for the future, do we really want to design an over-all Federal-state-local tax system in which — to put it in extremes — we dismantle the progressive and comparatively equitable Federal income tax while leaning ever more heavily on the regressive and comparatively inequitable state-local property, sales, and excise taxes? Or should we seek a system in which the powerful Federal income tax is used to support expenditures which otherwise either could not be made at all, or would have to be financed from regressive tax sources? My questions readily reveal my preferences.

Next, we encounter large disparities in economic and hence taxable capacity among the states which lead to perverse ratios in both state-local service levels and tax efforts; the wealthy states enjoy higher levels with less effort than the poorer states. For example, total state-local expenditures per capita in 1964 ranged from a high of $576 in Nevada to a low of $217 in South Carolina, a ratio of more than 2½ to 1. For public education, the range was from $201 in Utah to $91 in South Carolina, a ratio of more than 2 to 1. For public welfare, the highest per capita outlay is four times the lowest; for public health, it is five

times. Even when we take the average of the highest five
and the lowest five states in the various expenditure categories, the disparities are large and distressing:[18]

	General Expenditures	Education	Public Welfare	Health & Hospital
Highest Five	$511.96	$197.03	$52.58	$38.56
Lowest Five	252.40	94.17	14.97	14.34

The perversity of these ratios grows not only out of the
obvious concentration of low-income families in the low-
income states, but from the higher ratio of dependent
population to working-age population in those states. In
1959–60, the ten states with the highest ratios of dependent
population ranked among the lowest in per capita income,
and vice versa.[19]

Turning to the tax side, one finds that the richest states
— even though they make less "tax effort" — raise twice
as much revenue per capita from their own sources as the
poorest states. In 1964, the five top states in terms of per
capita revenue collections (New York, Nevada, California,
Wyoming, and Washington) collected $396 per capita
against $197 per capita in the five bottom states (South
Carolina, Arkansas, Mississippi, Alabama, and Kentucky).
Yet tax effort in the poor states is somewhat greater than
in the rich: while the ten richest states realized their revenue bounty with only a 12-percent tax burden as a percentage of personal income, the ten poorest states drew their
meager ration from a 13-percent tax burden.[20]

The general conclusion that the poorer states are on the
average making a greater effort in terms of tax-to-income
ratios than the richer states — and getting a much poorer

diet of governmental services for their pains — is a serious indictment of the workings of our fiscal federalism.

If the state and local governments are forced to solve their fiscal problems at the lowest common denominator arising out of interstate competition, limited jurisdiction, and inequality, their tax structures will deteriorate, and their vigor will be sapped. Without greater Federal help, they will face a disheartening battle for higher, and highly unpopular, taxes. That battle, combined with their inability to provide the services expected of enlightened governments in an affluent society, could seriously weaken their role in our federalism.

The inability of state and local governments to deal with the social and economic disaster of the 1930's was a severe blow to their prestige and influence. Since World War II, their quantitative role has been growing steadily. Indeed, they can lay claim to being the country's greatest "growth industry." Their expenditures have expanded more rapidly than those of any other major sector of the economy, public or private.

But rising responsibilities are not necessarily synonymous with rising strength. Whether greater activity leads to growing vitality depends on the flow of ideas, energy, and imagination applied in coping with these responsibilities. That, in turn, requires a sufficient flow of money to command the services of competent and imaginative people and to provide them with the funds to carry out their ideas. How far the revitalization process goes will depend on the financial and intellectual resources that state and local governments can command. Improvements are being made, and the caliber of state-local administration is rising. We need to accelerate that process.

What this calls for is not some senseless sacrifice of essential Federal authority on the altar of "states' rights," but a fiscal realignment that will simultaneously promote essential national interests and strengthen state-local capacity to serve without undermining the state-local will and capacity to govern.

In an era when painful fiscal pressures at the state-local level coexist with pleasant fiscal dividends at the Federal level, state and local governments have a commanding case (Vietnam aside) for stronger Federal financial support — in a form that will help redress the Federal-state-local fiscal balance *and* maintain the autonomy and strength of the states.

BEYOND GRANTS-IN-AID

A consideration of ways and means of enlarging Federal support for states and their subdivisions should begin with a recognition of the powerful assist that they are already getting from Federal aid, tax cuts, and policies for sustained prosperity.

The rise in Federal aid to state and local governments (including loans and shared revenues as well as grants) has been little short of spectacular. From about $4 billion in fiscal 1957, such aids have grown to a programmed $14½ billion in fiscal 1967. And they now represent one tenth of total Federal cash payments to the public, double their proportion a decade ago.

Less direct is the state-local bounty derived from huge tax cuts in a slack economy. An estimated $3 billion extra a year is flowing into state-local coffers from the 1964 income tax cut alone, a 7-percent increase for both state and local tax revenues. Most of this comes from economic expansion generated by the tax reduction. But some comes from the direct additions to the tax base of the nineteen income tax states that allow Federal income taxes as a deduction. The broad excise tax cuts of 1965 provided further stimulus and presumably opened some opportunities for states to rush in where the Federal angel no longer treads. Yet the list of attractive opportunities growing out of the excise tax reductions proved to be surprisingly short.

The ever-firmer commitment of the Federal government to maintain a high-employment, high-growth economy under the Employment Act of 1946 provides a firmer base for the states' and localities' own fiscal efforts. They can afford to be less fearful of repeated recessions, and they can count on higher average revenue yields at any given level of tax rates. Also both the management of Federal economic policy, which requires timely declaration of fiscal dividends, and the results of successful policy, which keep Federal coffers full, provide a favorable setting for more generous support to the states. This is reflected partly in the great growth of Federal aid, and partly in the new emphasis on "creative federalism" — for example, on the sharing of money and responsibility with community groups in the poverty program, with various state and local units in the fields of air and water purification, mass transportation, and urban development, and with municipal authorities under the proposed Demonstration Cities program.[21]

As we parcel out future fiscal dividends, grants-in-aid will be near the head of the queue. Conditional grants for specific functions play an indispensable role in our federalism. They unite Federal financing with state-local performance in a fiscal marriage of convenience, necessity, and opportunity:

• *convenience*, because they enable the Federal government to single out and support those state and local services in which there is an identified national interest. I have in mind particularly those services, like education and health, whose benefits in a country with a mobile people spill over into communities and states other than those in which they are performed. Functional aids enable the Federal government to put a financial floor under the level of specific services that is consistent with our national goals and priorities.

• *necessity*, because without this financial support the states and municipalities would be unable to meet the demands on them for essential services. Failure to meet these demands would eventually mean yielding the functions to the Federal government and thus weakening the fabric of federalism.

• *opportunity*, because putting the grants in conditional form enables the Federal government to apply national minimum standards, ensure financial participation at the state and local levels through matching requirements, and take both fiscal need and fiscal capacity into account.

But, on several counts, virtue gives some ground to vice. The aids that so admirably serve the national purpose may put state-local finance at cross purposes. In drawing on a limited supply of resources to finance and staff particular functions, the matching grant tends to siphon them away from the nonaided programs. And the poorer the state, the greater the tax effort that must be made to achieve any given amount of matching, and hence the less that is left over for the nonaided functions. To some extent, then, the state-local government trades fiscal freedom for fiscal strength.

Federal grants to serve highly specialized objectives have proliferated in recent years.[22] And once established, they do not yield gracefully to change or abolition. Unless this trend is reversed, Federal aids may weave a web of particularism, complexity, and Federal direction which will significantly inhibit a state's freedom of movement. The picture of Gulliver and the Lilliputians comes to mind.

We must move toward broader categories that will give states and localities more freedom of choice, more scope for expressing their varying needs and preferences, within the framework of national purpose.

Perhaps we should replace our myriad categories of educational aids with broad classes such as elementary, secondary, and higher education. Or perhaps the Elementary-Secondary Education Act of 1965, which goes against the tide of particularism, points the way. Funds under this act are distributed in proportion to the number of school children in low-income families. Within the general requirement that monies are to be applied to the needs of educationally deprived children, considerable latitude is allowed local and state boards of education to formulate specific plans.

Federal aids have risen from about 3 percent of state-local revenues in the 1920's, to 10 percent in the late 1940's, and 15 percent in 1965–66. This trend will and should continue. We have reached the point, though, where some restructuring of our system of Federal aids — some movement toward less conditional and less specific grants — is needed to maximize their contribution to the national interest not only in strong services but in a strong federalism.

But the conditional grant for specific purposes, for all its good works and even in its optimal form, falls short of the full fiscal needs of our federalism. Part of this is simply a recognition that even the rapid expansion of aids now in prospect will not enable state and local governments to make ends meet on acceptable terms. Part of it is that they need help in financing their nonaided functions — and it is only right that the Federal government temper the wind to the lambs it has shorn. And part of it is that the conditional grants are not well-suited to serve the intangible objectives of greater self-reliance and over-all vitality in state and local government. What we seek, then, are major new "methods of channeling Federal revenues to states and localities which will reinforce their independence while enlarging their capacity to serve their citizens." [23]

Such new methods must run the gauntlet of the several demanding criteria that emerge from our examination of the fiscal problems of federalism. Ideally, any new plan or approach should supply Federal funds to the states in ways that will (a) not only relieve immediate pressures on state-local treasuries, but hitch their fiscal wagon to the star of economic growth; (b) improve the distribution of Federal-state-local fiscal burdens; (c) reduce economic inequalities and fiscal disparities among the states; (d) stimulate state and local tax efforts; and (e) build up the vitality, efficiency, and fiscal independence of state and local governments.

The device that can serve all of these ends at once is yet to be found. But I believe that per capita revenue sharing, or some allied form of unfettered general assistance, will come closer to doing so than any alternative proposed thus far.[24] In explaining and appraising the revenue-sharing proposal, I will of course be making a case. Yet that case should be interpreted less as a defense of a particular plan than as a brief for a general approach.

PER CAPITA REVENUE SHARING

A forerunner of this device was used in the days of Andrew Jackson. With his acquiescence, Congress declared fiscal dividends to the states in 1837 out of the embarrassingly large Federal surplus produced by customs duties and proceeds of Federal sales of public lands. Funds remaining after the national debt was retired were distributed to the states in proportion to their respective numbers of congressmen and senators — a reasonable approximation of a per capita allocation. The distributions were made without restriction as to purpose but were formally not a grant. They were "put out on deposit" — but never recalled.

After the third installment, the surplus — and the "grants" — disappeared in the recession of 1838.

From that date to this only sporadic attention — and no action — has been accorded the general-purpose grant. Yet a whole family of synonyms has been spawned by various observers to identify this form of assistance. Unrestricted, unencumbered, unconditional, general-assistance, untied, no-strings, and block grants are among the candidates for the christening if this blessed fiscal event should one day occur. My own choice is "revenue sharing," mainly to distinguish the proposed financial assistance sharply from our existing grants-in-aid, with "per capita" added to differentiate it from proposals to rebate a share of the income tax to the states of origin.

THE PLAN

In capsule, the revenue-sharing plan would distribute a specified portion of the Federal individual income tax to the states each year on a per capita basis, with next to no strings attached. This distribution would be over and above existing and future conditional grants.

Form and amount of set-aside. The Federal government would each year set aside and distribute to the states 1 to 2 percent of the Federal individual income tax base (the amount reported as net taxable income by all individuals). This would mean that, under its existing rate schedule running from 14 to 70 percent, the Federal government would collect, say, 2 percentage points in each bracket for the states and 12 to 68 percentage points for itself. In 1966, for example, 2 points would have yielded the states

$5.6 billion, or 10 percent of the total Federal personal income tax collections of about $56 billion for the year.

The plan would relate the states' share to the Federal income tax base rather than to the income tax revenues, for the following reasons. First, taxable income is somewhat more stable than revenues. Second, since the states' share would be independent of the level and structure of Federal rates, this approach would not create a vested interest in a particular set of rates (though it might do so in exemption levels). Third, for the same reason, it is less likely to interfere with Federal use of the income tax in stabilization policy than a plan keyed to income tax revenues.

Trust fund. The sums collected for the states would be placed in a trust fund from which periodic distributions would be made. The trust fund would be the natural vehicle for handling such earmarked funds just as it is in the case of payroll taxes for social security purposes and motor vehicle and gasoline taxes for the highway program. It would also underscore the fact that the states receive the funds as a matter of right, free from the uncertainties and hazards of the annual appropriation process. Thus removed from the regular budget process, the revenue-sharing program would be less likely to encroach on the flow of grants-in-aid. Being cast in the form of a flow-through of income tax collections to the states, it would be more likely to come at the expense of income tax reductions.

Distribution of funds. The states would share the income tax proceeds on the basis of population. Per capita sharing would transfer some funds from states with high incomes — and therefore high per capita income tax liabilities —

to low-income, low-tax states. If the modest equalization implicit in per capita sharing were deemed too limited, a percentage — say 10 to 20 percent — could be set aside for supplements to states with low per capita income, or a high incidence of poverty, dependency, or urbanization.

Whether to leave the fiscal claims of the localities to the mercies of the political process and the institutional realities of each state or to require a pass-through to them is difficult to decide. I will examine this issue a bit further on.

Strings. States would be given wide latitude — nearly complete freedom — in the use of their revenue shares. Without sullying the basic no-strings character of these grants, one would ask the states to meet the usual public auditing, accounting, and reporting requirements on public funds; one would, of course, apply Title VI of the Civil Rights Act; one could even broadly restrict the use of the funds to education, health, welfare, and community development programs — or, at least, provide that they not be spent for highways (which are already financed by a special trust fund). But with the exception of the highway ban, I doubt that such limitations as to function are desirable in principle since the purpose of revenue-sharing is to enlarge the states' area of fiscal discretion. And, given the fungibility of money, such restrictions would be even less effective in practice.

Those who fear that some states will simply use the revenue shares to rest on their fiscal oars would put in a further condition: that the shares of those states which lowered their fiscal effort would be reduced.

ISSUES AND ALTERNATIVES

The revenue-sharing concept has not lacked for public discussion and for official attention, especially in state houses and in the halls of Congress.[25] Calls to action are necessarily muted by the heavy fiscal demands of Vietnam. But debate over the merits and limitations of the revenue-sharing approach has not been stilled.[26] It continues in the context of the rapid automatic growth of Federal revenues in an expanding economy — a growth that will involve the declaration of large fiscal dividends in the future — and that may even require special dividends after Vietnam, or in the even happier context of international disarmament.

What commends the revenue-sharing plan to its friends is primarily its simplicity; its provision of a large and automatically growing source of revenue to the states; the freedom of movement it offers the states; the consequent relief from gradual hardening of the categories under the conditional grants program; and its contribution to the vitality and self-determination that will make the states stronger partners in our federalism. Its supporters also cite the equalizing fiscal effects of the revenue-sharing plan and its effectiveness in maintaining a progressive distribution of Federal-state-local fiscal burdens.

Its doubters and detractors express fears that it will drain funds from higher priority national purposes which could be financed directly from the Federal budget; that these funds will go into leaky state purses; that a generous Federal revenue share will lead to a relaxation of state-local fiscal efforts; and that it will not meet the vital needs of local government, particularly in the central cities and metropolitan areas.

Revenue sharing as a source of state-local revenue. A share in Federal income tax revenues would be a share in the nation's economic growth. The Federal individual income tax base will reach the $300 billion mark in 1967. So each percent of the base would provide the states with $3 billion (and would cost the Federal government about 5 percent of its individual income tax revenues). Within five years, that amount would grow to roughly $4¼ billion (assuming a 6-percent annual growth in money GNP, and the income tax base growing 20 percent faster than GNP). If the plan were to start at 2 percent, it would channel to the states $6 billion a year, a sum roughly equivalent to one year's growth in state-local expenditures. The competing claims of Federal tax cuts and expenditure increases would probably require that the plan start more modestly (perhaps at one half of 1 percent or 1 percent) and build up gradually to 2 percent over three or four years. This gradual build-up would enable the states to program their own fiscal affairs more efficiently.

If 1 percent of the Federal income tax base were distributed in 1967, the grant would be roughly $15 per capita. This would mean, for example, grants of about $30 million for Arkansas, $280 million for California, $30 million for Colorado, $160 million for Illinois, $85 million for Massachusetts, $55 million for Louisiana and Minnesota, $10 million for Montana, $280 million for New York, $75 million for North Carolina, $180 million for Pennsylvania,

$15 million for Utah, $65 million for Virginia, and $60 million for Wisconsin.

In order to protect the states against cyclical downturns of revenue, it has been suggested that some sort of safeguard or minimum allotment — perhaps equivalent to the previous year's allocation — be provided in the plan. The trust fund could build up a modest reserve for such contingencies. The postwar experience does not suggest any great need for such a safeguard. In spite of four recessions, the grants under the proposed plan would have risen in every year since 1949. The income tax base, to which the allotments are keyed, has grown from $65 billion in 1946 to $128 billion in 1955, to $210 billion in 1963, and the estimated $300 billion in 1967 — and has risen from 31 percent of GNP in 1946 to an estimated 38 percent in 1967.

It also goes without saying — or at least I thought it did — that the Federal commitment to share income tax revenues with the states would be a contractual one, good through thick and thin, through surplus and deficit in the Federal budget. But since privately circulated memoranda have labeled the plan "surplus grants," and pounced on its supposedly fatal flaw of being payable only when the Federal government has a surplus, it is perhaps worth underscoring the obvious in this case. The plan would hardly have its claimed advantages of stiffening and strengthening state and local governments if they were last in the fiscal line, ever fearful that the revenue bounty might suddenly be withdrawn. The very nature of the proposal calls for them to be first in line for their modest share of the income tax, even if it means that the Federal government has to bear the brunt of periodic deficit financing — which, indeed, it can do much more readily and appropriately than state and local governments.

Although providing significant added support to the states, an allotment of 2 percent of the Federal income tax base would claim only a moderate share of the automatic revenue growth of Federal taxes. Viewing the matter from the perspective of late 1964, before Vietnam so rudely intervened, I visualized as a reasonable allocation of the prospective built-in Federal revenue growth of $35 billion between 1965 and 1970, the following: $5 billion for revenue sharing, $10 billion for tax cuts, and $20 billion for increased Federal spending (including grants-in-aid). This 5–10–20 strategy would have provided substantial and vital relief to the states without impairing the support for Federal functions or ignoring the claims for further tax reduction. Since that day, excise tax cuts, the intervention of Vietnam, and accelerated expansion and price increases have changed the numbers and the proportions. But the revenue power on which we can draw for such fiscal plans and dreams has grown, not shrunk.

Distributive impact. Per capita revenue sharing would serve the ends of both political and economic democracy: political democracy, by its contribution — in the form of a reliable and rising flow of funds to the states, free of onerous controls — to a more decentralized and pluralistic society; economic democracy, by helping to preserve a progressive Federal-state-local tax system, to support progressive state-local expenditures, and to promote interstate equalization — in short, by contributing to equality of economic opportunity.

It is politically realistic, I believe, to assume that the revenue shares set aside for the states would absorb funds that otherwise would have gone mainly into Federal income tax reduction and partly into Federal expenditure increases. It would transform them mainly into increases in state-local expenditures and partly into a slowdown of state-local tax increases.

With expenditure demands on state and local governments rising by 7 to 8 percent a year, the fiscal dividends from the Federal government would not often go into tax reduction. And if, in part, they did result in slower increases in sales, property, and excise taxes — or even in an occasional cut in such taxes — I do not view this as original fiscal sin. Who is prepared to say that slowing down the reduction of the progressive and relatively equitable Federal income tax in order to relieve pressure on regressive, inequitable, and inefficient property and consumer taxes is a bad trade? Dollar for dollar, substituting lower state-local taxes for cuts in Federal taxes would increase the progressivity of the tax system — and benefit the economy by the relative shift away from taxes that bear unevenly on consumers and heavily on business costs. Full use of the shared revenue for higher state-local expenditures would, of course, have an even more progressive effect since their benefits are heavily weighted toward the lower income groups.

Detailed statistical estimates of the distribution of tax burdens and expenditure benefits at the Federal and state-local levels bear out these conclusions.[27] State-local tax burdens rise gently with income in the lowest income brackets — from an estimated 12 percent of family income below $2,000 to 18 percent in the $4,000 to $5,000 income bracket. But from there on up the income scale, they regress with a vengeance — dropping to 6 percent on incomes of $10,000 and over. Property and sales taxes are, as expected, the villain of the piece, taking an estimated 17 percent of income in the $4,000 to $5,000 bracket, but plunging to only 4 percent for incomes over $10,000. Federal tax burdens, in contrast, run from 18 percent of family incomes below $2,000 to 31 percent over $10,000 (though not without a surprising dip for incomes between $5,000 and $10,000).

Both Federal and state-local expenditures are progressive in their incidence ("progressive" here meaning that they benefit the lower income groups more than the higher). The state-local expenditure pattern is strongly so, declining steadily from an estimated 43 percent of income for the poorest families to 6 percent for families with incomes above $10,000.[28] The ratio of Federal expenditure benefits to income also drops as income rises, but less sharply and steadily: from 42 percent of the poorest incomes to 17 percent of incomes over $10,000.

These estimates are subject to important limitations of data and concept. Yet study after study has confirmed the unmistakable pattern of substantially progressive Federal taxes and expenditures, strongly regressive state-local taxes, and strongly progressive state-local expenditures. They settle no questions of social priority or of efficiency in taxing and spending. But they leave no doubt that a shift of revenues to the states and localities would make our over-all fiscal system more progressive.

Interstate equalization. Per capita revenue sharing would have a significant interstate equalizing effect, an effect that could readily be magnified by simple adjustments in the sharing formula. As already noted, distributing 2 percent of the individual income tax base in 1967 on a straight population basis would return $30 per capita to all of the states. Yet the 2 percent would draw $42 per capita from the ten richest states and only about $18 from the ten poorest (using 1964 Internal Revenue data adjusted to the projected $300-billion income tax base in 1967).

This, by the way, gives us a measure of the difference between per capita revenue sharing and sharing on the basis of origin. The latter would return the same $42 to the richest states and $18 to the poorest states that came from those states. In this respect, the Federal crediting device — credits against Federal tax for state income taxes paid — is similar to sharing the income tax on the basis of origin.

In contrast, conditional grants-in-aid lend themselves to formulas that can take fiscal capacity into account. A number of the functional aid programs provide larger unit grants to the low-income than to the high-income states. But aggregate data on Federal aid are a disappointment on this score. For example, in 1964, Federal grants (including highway grants) to the ten lowest-income states averaged $58 per capita, to the ten highest, $85 per capita. As a percentage of state-local general revenues, the grants represented 21 percent for the ten lowest-income states and just under 20 percent for the ten highest. These figures suggest that even though individual programs may have an equalizing effect, the over-all impact is not equalizing unless one takes into account the geographical incidence of the Federal taxes from which the grants are financed.[29]

As suggested earlier, the per capita formula could be adjusted to take special account of the urgent needs of the poorest states. If as little as 15 percent of the total funds were to be set aside for distribution to the lowest-income third of the states, it would mean raising the grant to the poorest state by perhaps two and one-half times the amount that it would get from the straight per capita formula. The easy adaptability of the revenue-sharing plan to almost any preference as to equalization among the states can be an important asset.

State-local tax effort and Federal tax credits. Some misgivings have been expressed about the revenue-sharing plan on grounds that it contains no spur to greater state-local tax effort and might even encourage the states to relax their fiscal efforts. In the preceding section I have suggested that the distributive implications of some letup in fiscal effort would not be unfavorable. But this is not to say that greater effort, and particularly greater equality of effort, should not be encouraged.

The revenue-sharing formula could be modified to take account of fiscal effort and thereby not only discourage backsliding but provide a positive stimulus to greater and more equal tax effort. "A simple and effective way of allowing for effort would be to weight the per capita grants by the ratio of state to average tax effort in the country, where tax effort is defined as the ratio of state-local general revenues to personal income." [30] States whose tax efforts are below par or who cut their taxes in response to the Federal subsidy would be penalized by reduction in their allotments. States making a high fiscal effort or intensifying that effort would be rewarded with larger allotments.

Under the suggested measure of effort, as it would have applied in 1964, Louisiana, New Mexico, and North Dakota had effort indexes of 120 or above. Eleven other states had indexes of 110 or more: Arizona, California, Hawaii, Idaho, Minnesota, Mississippi, Montana, South Dakota, Washington, Wisconsin, and Wyoming. At the lower end, nine states had an effort index of only 85 or less: Connecticut, Delaware, Illinois, Maryland, Missouri, New Jersey, Ohio, Pennsylvania, and Virginia.[31]

Since such an effort index would make inroads on the simplicity of the plan, one is somewhat loath to recommend it. Without it, however, the plan would have to concede superiority on this score to the tax crediting device. The excellent proposal for an income tax credit advanced by the Advisory Commission on Intergovernmental Relations in 1966 effectively demonstrates this advantage.[32] Under its proposal, the taxpayer would be allowed to credit against his Federal individual income tax liability a substantial percentage — 40 percent seems to be the preferred rate — of his state income tax payments. (Taxpayers in the very high brackets, for whom deductibility of the state tax against the Federal taxable income provides a larger tax saving, would retain such deductibility as an alternative to the credit.) The Commission's tax credit plan would put substantial funds at the state's disposal — about $800 million a year at today's tax rates, with a maximum of perhaps $3.5 billion a year in the foreseeable future as the credit led to more widespread and intensive use of the income tax by the states.

The Commission recommendation is an ingenious variation on income tax credit ideas that go back many decades. In the more traditional form, the credit would be taken — as in the case of the estate tax — as a specified proportion, say 10 percent, of the Federal tax, and no more. The effect of this more traditional plan is to relieve the taxpayer of all state tax liability up to the stated percentage of the Federal tax, and none above that point. The Commission plan has the great attraction of being open-ended. No matter how high the rates of a state income tax may be pushed, 40 percent of that tax is, in effect, automatically paid by the Federal government in the form of a tax offset.[33]

The major attractions of the Commission's tax credit plan are that it would not only put large sums into the states' hands to be utilized entirely as they see fit, but would give them a major incentive to use our best form of taxation. But the plan is also subject to some limitations.

First, unlike the revenue-sharing plan, a considerable part of the tax credit in the thirty-three income tax states would initially be a direct benefit to the taxpayers rather than to their governments — though this initial relief would eventually be dwarfed by higher tax liabilities if the credit had its intended stimulative effect.

Second, as noted above, the tax crediting device provides no interstate equalization of fiscal burdens.

Third, the plan faces the tough pragmatic barrier that seventeen states at present have no income tax, some of them because of seemingly stubborn constitutional prohibitions. This barrier, more than any other, has kept the tax credit idea languishing in textbooks, monographs, and doctoral theses (including my own of twenty-five years ago) for many decades. Although the tax credit is meant to offer the states an enlightened helping hand, some of them will regard it as coercion rather than cooperation.

Many of us, I am sure, share the underlying conviction that the states should be making far more use of the income tax — particularly the personal income tax — than they are today. In addition to the seventeen states without income taxes, twelve impose a tax that amounts to less than 1 percent of Federal adjusted gross income; another twelve have income tax burdens under 2 percent; and only nine have effective rates, in this sense, of over 2 percent — ranging to a maximum of over 3 percent in Delaware, Oregon, and Wisconsin.[34] A form of Federal fiscal support which would lead the states into these green pastures of growth and progression that they are now so widely neglecting has an understandably strong attraction.

States seeking broad grants derived from the Federal income tax should ask whether their case may not suffer from having such a spotty record in their own utilization of this excellent source. Some of the advocates of the income tax credit have argued that it would induce (a much nicer word than "coerce") the states into a stronger position to lay claim to a share of Federal income tax revenue. Indeed, in the best of all worlds, one would hope to be able to afford both the income tax credit and revenue sharing. If a choice has to be made, the balance of advantages seems to favor the revenue-sharing plan. But the income tax credit would be a major advance in Federal-state fiscal relations, a very good second best. Those of us who labor in the vineyards of Federal-state fiscal relations should take care that the good becomes the handmaiden, not the enemy, of the best.

The claims of local governments. Per capita revenue sharing would miss its mark if it did not serve to relieve some of the intense fiscal pressures on local governments, especially in urban areas. The question is whether this relief would come automatically from a no-strings grant, or whether a specific part of the trust fund should be reserved for the local units.

The case for leaving this to the discretion of the states is based on several rather persuasive arguments. Directing that a specified percentage or amount should go to the localities might encumber the plan with the rigidities it is designed to avoid. States differ greatly in their division of responsibilities and finances between state and local governments. In some states as much as two thirds of total state-local expenditures may be financed by the state government. In other states the opposite ratio may apply. Arrangements for state aids and shared taxes differ greatly, and there are substantial variations in the division of functional responsibilities as well.

At the same time it is true that all states, in one way or

another, raise sizable amounts of revenue for their local subdivisions. Over half of the general expenditures of the states takes the form of transfers to local governments. The states supply something like two fifths of the funds spent by local governments for education. All told, nearly a third of local general revenues comes from the states. Small wonder, then, that we typically hyphenate "state-local." We have little reason to fear, I believe, that the shared income tax revenues would simply be bottled up at the state level. This does not, of course, resolve the question whether *enough* would pass through to local, and especially urban, units of government.

Here, as an article of faith, I count rather heavily on reapportionment to achieve equity in the allocation of funds within the states. Yet I do not wish to say that reapportionment, for all its good works, is a guarantee of the balanced distribution of Federal funds. Central cities will be represented in proportion to their population but not to their problems. For their crushing problems of poverty, racial disability, obsolete social capital, and undernourished public services cannot be solved within their own bounds. They require recognition — and financial help — on a metropolitan-area, a state, and a national basis. The danger that growing suburban representation under reapportionment will still leave state legislatures unsympathetic to the problems of the core cities argues for some adjustment in the allocation formula to give special recognition to their needs.

Indeed, were it possible, one would want to recognize the attractions of both metropolitan-area and regional approaches to the solution of governmental problems by some form of special stimulants in the allocation formula. Yet, if the revenue-sharing plan is to retain its advantages of flexibility — the freedom to put funds to the neediest uses as each state sees them — then the less arbitrary and fixed the pattern of distribution, the better. Perhaps the special claims of urban areas, metropolitan government, and regionalism will have to be the subject of special programs such as the Appalachia regional development program, the Demonstration Cities program, and the community action programs under the Economic Opportunity Act.

One possibility in the revenue-sharing arrangement would be to put a floor under the pass-through from the states to the localities by specifying that no less than the present ratio of state financing of local services be maintained. The Javits bill meets this problem by requiring that the states must distribute to their local governments an equitable proportion of their allotments — the ratio in each state is to be no less than the average of the state's distribution of its own revenues to local governments over the previous five years.[35] Again, of course, in attempting to enforce such a provision, one faces the perennial problem of fungibility: the states might dutifully conform to the pass-through requirements of the revenue-sharing law and simultaneously reduce other payments to the local governments.

The pass-through issue is a perplexing one. Seemingly persuasive considerations can be brought to bear on both sides of the question. How to give special weight to the claims of central cities and metropolitan areas, yet not freight the formula with too many conditions, remains a challenge to ingenuity.

National purpose. However one might resolve the important questions of distribution, equalization, tax effort, and pass-throughs, one has to come back to the jugular question of the impact of the revenue sharing or general-assistance grants on the fabric of federalism. Would the national purpose — the quest for a physical and social environment that will enhance the life of man — be served well or ill? Would we, as some think, be playing into the hands of waste and corruption, or would efficiency and better government be the outcome? And, finally, would the vitality and quality of the states — and hence the strength of federalism — be sapped or strengthened?

Some critics fear that turning revenues over to the states without Federal controls would sacrifice national priorities, drain funds away from high-priority education, urban renewal, and mass housing programs toward low-priority uses. This danger is, I believe, greatly overrated.

Not only is the proposed revenue share small in relation to the total Federal budget, but even at the $6 billion level, it would be less than one year's automatic growth in Federal revenues. And in the form of a direct collection of a specified share of the income tax on the states' behalf, routed through a trust fund, the aid to the states would, as already noted, come chiefly at the expense of income tax cuts, not Federal civilian programs.

Further, the defenders of these programs have some impressive advantages in the battle for funds. Federal organization, whether in the executive agencies, in the budget process, or in the congressional committees, is largely along functional lines. Private interest groups and pressures operate along the same lines. Speak of schools, highways, farm subsidies, or health programs — and groups in the Administration, Congress, and private life spring to the colors and man the budgetary battle stations.

But speak of bolstering and revitalizing state and local governments, and who listens? Or, at least, whose attention span goes beyond a day or two? What troops can state-local governments command in the political and fiscal wars? Few enough, even with the welcome new emphasis on creative federalism, to lead me to believe that general-assistance grants would be but a minor threat to either the well-fortified positions or the further conquests of the functional programs. This is not to say that these programs have things all their own way, that they get all the money they need. But I doubt that revenue sharing would drain funds from them. Indeed, it would better equip the states to hold up their end of the job, both in the broad sense of making them more effective units of government and in the narrow sense of enabling them to meet the matching requirements of the functional grants. In other words, minimum-strings assistance to the states would serve, not thwart, the national purpose.

This conviction is strengthened by even a brief review of the uses to which the states have, in recent years, put added funds (85 percent of which, one should recall, come from their own sources). Of the $37 billion increase in expenditures of states and localities from 1954 to 1964, 41 percent went into education. Another 14 percent of the increase went into health and welfare. Highways took 16 percent; police, fire, and sanitation, 8 percent; natural resources and community development, 4 percent. Only 3 percent of the increase went for general administration; 4 percent for increased service on debt; and 10 percent for other purposes.

Most striking about this list is that — even before long-overdue general school aid was coaxed out of Congress by President Johnson in 1965 — the states and localities put their greatest single effort into education. Who would fault them on this sense of priority? But let me move from defense to offense. Vital as the Great Society programs are in turning abundance to the nation's good, it does not follow that government's contribution to the good life comes exclusively with a "Made in Washington" label. Many of the seemingly humdrum functions of state-local governments, undertaken with little or no Federal help, come pretty close to the heart of our national purpose. Police protection and law enforcement, elementary sanitation, recreation facilities, street maintenance and lighting — things that, together with housing and schooling, spell the difference between a decent and a squalid environment, a respectable neighborhood and an explosive ghetto — are cases in point. We neglect them at our peril.

Efficiency and honesty. Aside from the question of priorities, critics charge that state-local government is so often inefficient, wasteful, and corrupt that it is unworthy of anything but tightly controlled Federal support. The issue of honesty and efficiency takes both crude and subtle forms.

In its crudest form, the charge is that many state legislatures are dominated by corrupt, venal, and interest-ridden buccaneers; that state administrations are weak and incompetent; that local government is archaic in structure and poorly managed. On each point one has to begin by granting that horrible examples can be found to fit each of these charges, and that state and local governments have not done nearly enough to overcome obsolete structure and ineffective administration.

But we must be careful not to condemn by cliché. Not only does reapportionment promise better balance and new blood in legislatures — and hence fairer and more intelligent allocation of funds — but the picture of administrative incompetence is greatly overdrawn. As one keen observer put it after mingling with governors and their staffs for several days at the National Governors' Conference, "The great majority of the Governors . . . are dedicated, hardworking, and above all, highly competent individuals, handling complex administrative and policy problems that would overwhelm many a Senator." He went on to say that "for the most part, too, these men are surrounded by trained, talented staffs, not mere political cronies and hangers-on." [36]

Part of the answer to the critics must be found also in the basic objective of general-purpose grants. It is precisely to enable the states to overcome some of their weaknesses that broad-gauged grants are so badly needed. Denying the states such assistance would perpetuate the evils that are not simply in the eye of the beholders.

Revenue sharing could contribute to efficiency by relaxing the ever-tighter grip of special-purpose aids. True, these aids have created islands of personnel competence and administrative efficiency. Nonetheless, with over eighty special-purpose grants now in force the system not only becomes complex and uncoordinated, but also tends to interfere with an efficient allocation of public funds, especially in poorer states. Under the whiplash of matching, funds may be driven away from nonaided but possibly higher-priority, and hence more efficient, uses. To avoid an inefficient allocation of state-local funds, our system of tightly tied aids needs to be flanked by wide-latitude grants like those provided by revenue-sharing. The Federal aid system would thereby gain in balance and rationality, and the states would gain in efficiency and freedom of choice.

Some fears of inefficiency rest on grounds, not that the vessels into which Federal funds would be poured are cracked and leaky, but that monies flowing in without the pain of self-taxation or the penalty of Federal controls would be spent like water. Yet it is difficult to see why the proposed sharing of revenues with the states should promote loose spending. First, the Federal funds, unmarked by any radioactive tracers, would be commingled with state and local funds. Second, they would cover only a modest percentage of the cost of any given program; the bulk of the funds would be the community's own hard-earned tax money. Third, since the flow of receipts each year would be fixed, there would be none of the incentive to profligacy that arises when the spender knows that "there's always more where that came from." All told, there is little reason to believe that states and localities would spend the money less wisely, efficiently, and responsibly than funds from their own sources.

One of the false issues of efficiency that besets the debate is the perennial charge that channeling Federal funds to the states increases government costs by "the additional freight of a round-trip to Washington." This charge would hardly merit serious debate were it not such a stubborn weed in the garden of fiscal coordination. Yet it should wither before the facts. First, costs of collecting Federal taxes are far below costs of collecting state and local taxes. Second, given vast advantages in jurisdiction, size, and scale, the Internal Revenue Service is an inherently more efficient tax administering agency than those of the states. Third, with respect to plans like revenue sharing, there would need to be no new machinery and no added administrative costs of any consequence. The round-trip to Washington would cost less than a round-trip to the state house or city hall. On these, admittedly narrow, efficiency grounds, the flow-through of Federal income tax funds to the states would get high marks.

In view of the Federal government's vastly superior taxing power and efficiency — in taxation, the whole *is* greater than the sum of its parts — why not turn over the entire taxing job to it? The obvious answer is that state-local government would then be completely dependent on the power of the Federal purse. As citizens, we are willing to pay a considerable premium for independent taxation as a cost of self-government at the state-local level. At the same time we seek the strength which can come from alloying such taxation with Federal grants that share the revenue bounties of prosperity with the governments which bear its burden.

Revitalizing the states. Transcending all other considerations, as we seek new forms of Federal fiscal relief for the states, is the need not simply to increase their resources but to restore their vitality; not simply to make them better "service stations" of federalism but to release their creative and innovative energies; not simply to pay lip service to "states' rights" but to give substance to local self-government.

State and local officials need a chance to worry, not just about getting the dead cat out of the alley — as Daniel Hoan, the socialist mayor of Milwaukee, once characterized the first demand on him after he had been elected to the exalted post of mayor — but about how we can more effectively devote our growing abundance to our common needs, how we can get at the roots of our social failures. They need an opportunity to worry not just about where the next dollar is coming from but what the world is coming to.

Money alone won't do it. We should not fall prey to what Senator Kenneth Keating once called "the Washington reflex," the tendency "to discover a problem and then to throw money at it, hoping that it will somehow go away." Some $14 billion of functional aids are serving high national purposes, but they have not made our state-local fiscal malaise go away. Nor is it likely to go away until we change the form and terms in which we furnish new Federal funds to the states.

Revenue sharing, or similar general-purpose grants, could supply the missing fiscal link. On one hand, the funds would not be tied to specified national interests, bound by detailed controls, forced into particular channels, and subject to annual Federal decisions. On the other, they would not have to be wrung out of a reluctant state-local tax base at great political risk to bold and innovative governors and legislators. In short, revenue sharing would provide a dependable flow of Federal funds in a form that would enlarge, not restrict, the options of state and local decision makers.

One readily visualizes the tangible benefits: higher salaries and hence higher caliber staffs; better performance of the jobs the Federal government subcontracts to states and localities; and a more effective attack on problems beyond the reach of Federal projects and the present system of Federal aids.

But the intangible gains are even more promising. General-assistance grants would offer relief from the intense fiscal pressures that lead to default and dependence; would help the nation tap not only the skills and knowledge but the wisdom and ingenuity of our state and local units; and would enable these units to flex their muscles and exercise greater discretion and responsibility. It would help them hold their heads high and fulfill their intended role as strong and resilient partners in our federalism.

The revenue-sharing plan, indeed the whole general-assistance approach, has been criticized from one side as too conservative and from the other as too liberal. It is said to be too conservative in that it interrupts the march of history toward centralization, toward increased power and responsibility for a Federal government which is efficient and well equipped to promote the national interest. Strengthening the states, in part at the risk of retarding the growth of Federal programs, is said to be a retrograde step.

It is said to be too liberal because it would redistribute some funds from higher to lower income groups by drawing them from the progressive Federal income tax and channeling them, through state budgets, largely into education, health, and welfare; and because it would levy more heavily on the wealthy states and share more generously with the poorer states.

But we can turn both of these points to the defense of revenue-sharing or similar plans: they combine the sound conservative principle of preserving the decentralization of power and intellectual diversity that are essential to a workable federalism with the compassionate liberal principle of promoting equality of opportunity among different income groups and regions of the United States. In turning these arguments to advantage, I am reminded that one dare not be any more doctrinaire on the political economy of federalism than on the political economy of stable prosperity.

I have been making a general case in terms of a particular plan. I believe that the plan would go to the heart of the fiscal problem of our federalism. But let me stress again that it is the general case, not the particular plan, that matters. The important thing is to be ready to move from talk to action once Vietnam relents — to harness Federal funds to state-local initiative as part of the national undertaking to convert economic growth into a better life. The good life will not come, ready-made, from some Federal assembly line. It has to be custom built, engaging the effort and imagination and resourcefulness of the community. Whatever fiscal plan is adopted must recognize this need.

No single fiscal plan can move the mountains back to Mohammed. But it will not be working alone. Other earth-moving, possibly even earth-shaking, forces are already at work. Reapportionment has already realigned thirty-five legislatures. New demands flooding in on the states and localities are stirring new efforts at administrative and legislative reform. A growing sense of social corrosion and crisis — of which Watts and Harlem and Chicago's South Side are explosive examples — is awakening a new sense of state and local responsibility. And sustained prosperity is opening new vistas of fiscal hope. New Federal efforts to stiffen the state-local fiscal spine would be made in the context of important forces already gathering for a renaissance of the states.

And here the linkage between the potential of our economy and the potential of our federalism comes into clear focus. The steps we take to strengthen the fiscal base of our federalism — partly by expanding and improving the existing system of Federal grants, partly by building on emerging institutions like the community action and Appalachia programs, and partly by developing new devices like revenue sharing — are all elements of a design to use our growing mastery of the economic environment to master also our physical and social environment. That design can give substance to the promise that our growing abundance will indeed be used "to serve our ultimate social objectives in a framework of freedom."

NOTES

INDEX

Notes

CHAPTER I: Advice and Consensus in Economic Policy Making

1. Employment Act of 1946, as amended (60 Stat. 23, Public Law 304, 79th Congress). Section 2 of the act directs the Federal government to use "all its plans, functions, and resources . . . to promote maximum employment, production, and purchasing power." Section 3 calls upon the President to specify the levels of activity prevailing in the U.S. economy, the levels expected and the levels needed to carry out the policy of the act. Section 4 creates the three-member Council of Economic Advisers in the Executive Office of the President and specifies its duties and functions. Section 5 establishes the Joint Economic Committee of the Congress.

The definitive study of the origin and passage of the Employment Act is by Stephen Kemp Bailey, *Congress Makes a Law: The Story Behind the Employment Act of 1946* (New York: Columbia University Press, 1950).

2. Remarks of President Lyndon B. Johnson at swearing-in ceremony for James Duesenberry, to be a member of the Council of Economic Advisers, February 2, 1966 (White House press release).

3. *Business Week*, February 5, 1966, p. 125.

4. For further discussion of the economist's way of looking at problems, see Kenneth E. Boulding, *The Skills of the Economist* (Toronto: Clarke, Irwin, 1958), especially chs. i and iv; and

Charles J. Hitch, "The Uses of Economics," in the Brookings Dedication Lectures, *Research for Public Policy* (Washington, D.C.: The Brookings Institution, 1961).

5. Arthur Okun, a member of the CEA, factored out the balance between inflationary pressures and capacity as follows: "A cutback in investment plans sufficient to moderate industrial production by 1 percent in the fourth quarter of 1966 would hold down capacity by no more than 0.2 percent. The resulting difference of nearly 1 percent in the average industrial operating rate . . . would be a big help in our efforts to prevent the fires of inflation." "Economic Prospects and Policies," remarks before the Society of American Business Writers, Minneapolis, Minnesota, May 10, 1966, p. 14 (CEA mimeographed release).

6. Leon H. Keyserling, "Aggregate or Structural Approaches to Achieving Employment Act Objectives," in *Twentieth Anniversary of the Employment Act of 1946: An Economic Symposium,* Joint Economic Committee, Congress of the United States, 89th Cong., 2nd Sess., February 23, 1966 (Washington, D.C.: G.P.O., 1966), pp. 19, 22.

7. This position is ably argued by George Stigler in "The Politics of Political Economists," *Quarterly Journal of Economics* 73:522–532 (November 1959).

8. Robert Dorfman, *The Price System* (Englewood Cliffs, N.J.: Prentice-Hall, 1964), p. 7.

9. As quoted in *Time,* December 31, 1965, p. 65.

10. American Institute of Public Opinion release, "Public Divided on Wage-Price 'Freeze,' " February 4, 1966. The release noted that "a similar question on wage-price controls asked only a few weeks after the start of the Korean War, in 1950, found a clear majority of 55 percent in favor of 'freezing' both prices and wages."

11. President Kennedy's deep concern over the persistent balance of payments deficit and its constraining influence in U.S. foreign affairs is vividly described by both Schlesinger and Sorensen in their books on Kennedy. Theodore C. Sorensen, *Kennedy* (New York: Harper & Row, 1965), pp. 405–412; Arthur M. Schlesinger, Jr., *A Thousand Days: John F. Kennedy in the White House* (Boston: Houghton Mifflin, 1965), pp. 654–655.

More generally, both books are indispensable in gaining an understanding of economic policy and economic advisers in the Kennedy Presidency. See especially chs. xvi and xvii in Sorensen and chs. xxiii and xxiv in Schlesinger. See also Hobart Rowen, *The Free Enterprisers: Kennedy, Johnson, and the Business Establishment* (New York: G. P. Putnam, 1964).

12. The role of the economist in government has been the subject of many articles and books. A recent probing study is by Edward S. Flash, Jr., *Economic Advice and Presidential Leadership: The Council of Economic Advisers* (New York: Columbia University Press, 1965). Earlier volumes of particular interest are *Economics and Public Policy* (Washington, D.C.: The Brookings Institution, 1955); and W. A. Jöhr and H. W. Singer, *The Role of The Economist as Official Adviser* (London: Allen & Unwin, 1955).

Among articles focusing on the American scene are Gardner Ackley, "The Contribution of Economists to Policy Formation," *The Journal of Finance* 21:169–177 (May 1966); Robert D. Calkins, "Economics as an Aid to Policy," Report to Management Publication Series, no. 9 (University of Southern California, August 1963); Charles Hitch, "The Uses of Economics" (together with panel comments by Francis M. Bator, Charles L. Schultze, and Charls E. Walker), in *Research for Public Policy* (Washington, D.C.: The Brookings Institution, 1961); E. A. Goldenweiser, "Research and Policy," *Federal Reserve Bulletin* 30:1–6 (April 1944); James Tobin, "The Intellectual Revolution in U.S. Economic Policy Making," Noel Buxton Lecture, University of Essex, England, January 18, 1966.

In the extensive literature on the subject in Great Britain, some of the most informative articles are Sir Robert Hall, "The Place of the Economist in Government," *Oxford Economic Papers* 7: 119–135 (June 1955), and "Reflections on the Practical Application of Economics," *Economic Journal* 69:639–652 (December 1959); A. K. Cairncross, "On Being an Economic Adviser," *Scottish Journal of Political Economy* 2:181–197 (October 1955); P. D. Henderson, "The Use of Economists in British Administration," *Oxford Economic Papers* 13:5–26 (February 1961); I. M. D. Little, "The Economist in Whitehall," *Lloyd's Bank Review*, no. 44

(April 1957), pp. 29–40; Ely Devons, "The Role of the Economist in Public Affairs," *Lloyd's Bank Review*, no. 53 (July 1959), pp. 26–38.

13. Employment Act of 1946, sec. 3.

14. Ackley, "The Contribution of Economists to Policy Formation," p. 176.

15. These concepts are spelled out in Chapter II.

16. As quoted in Norton E. Long, *The Polity* (Chicago: Rand McNally, 1962), p. 104.

17. Arthur Smithies, "Economic Welfare and Policy," in *Economics and Public Policy*, p. 1.

18. *Economic Report of the President, Transmitted to the Congress January 1962, Together With The Annual Report of the Council of Economic Advisers* (Washington, D.C.: G.P.O., 1962), p. 37. (Hereafter this will be referred to as either *Economic Report* or *Annual Report*, depending on which section is cited.)

19. President Lyndon B. Johnson, State of the Union Message, January 12, 1966.

20. *January 1961 Economic Report of the President and The Economic Situation and Outlook*, Hearings Before the Joint Economic Committee, Congress of the United States, 87th Cong., 1st Sess. (Washington, D.C.: G.P.O., 1961), p. 291. The varying conceptions of earlier Councils and their chairmen on responsibility toward the public, the Congress, and the President are examined in Flash's study (see note 12), in *The President's Economic Advisers* by Corinne Silverman, The Inter-University Case Program, no. 48 (University of Alabama Press, 1959), and in Edwin G. Nourse, *Economics in the Public Service: Administrative Aspects of the Employment Act* (New York: Harcourt, Brace, 1953).

21. Hearings Before the Joint Economic Committee (1961), p. 292.

22. Letter to the author, May 12, 1966.

23. Letter to the author, June 13, 1966.

24. Hugh Sidey, *John F. Kennedy, President: A Reporter's Inside Story* (New York: Atheneum, 1963), p. 378.

25. *Employment, Growth, and Price Levels*, Hearings Before the Joint Economic Committee, Congress of the United States, 86th Cong., 1st Sess. (Washington, D.C.: G.P.O., 1959), part 9A, p. 2988.

26. *The Polity*, pp. 97, 98. Long's perceptive chapter, "Popular Support for Government Economic Programs," foresaw many of the barriers of public misunderstanding and ideology that had to be overcome to realize the promise of the Employment Act of 1946. This chapter was first published as an article in 1948.

27. Arthur F. Burns, "Progress Toward Economic Stability," *American Economic Review* 50:1 (March 1960).

28. Seymour E. Harris, *Economics of the Kennedy Years* (New York: Harper & Row, 1964), p. 23.

29. President John F. Kennedy, State of the Union Message, January 30, 1961.

30. President John F. Kennedy, Special Message to the Congress: Program for Economic Recovery and Growth, February 2, 1961.

31. Hearings Before the Joint Economic Committee (1961), p. 361.

32. *The Economist*, November 13, 1965, p. 716.

33. Long, *The Polity*, p. 99.

34. Sorensen, *Kennedy*, p. 430.

35. These dangers are examined by Kermit Gordon in "Reflections on Spending," in *Public Policy*, published annually by the Graduate School of Public Administration, Harvard University, 1966, vol. XV.

36. Joseph Kraft, "Public Left in Fiscal Darkness," *Minneapolis Tribune*, June 21, 1966.

37. *Annual Report* (1962), pp. 185–190.

38. *Managing a Full Employment Economy: A CED Symposium on Problems of Maintaining Prosperity Without Inflation* (New York: Committee for Economic Development, 1966).

39. Bertrand de Jouvenel, "On the Evolution of Forms of Government," in de Jouvenel, ed., *Futuribles I* (Geneva: Librarie Droz, 1963). See also Neil W. Chamberlain, in *Private and Public Planning* (New York: McGraw-Hill, 1965), especially pp. 194–196; and Jacques Ellul, *The Technological Society* (New York: Alfred Knopf, 1965).

40. *Business Week*, March 5, 1966, p. 152.

41. Tobin, "Intellectual Revolution in U.S. Economic Policy Making," p. 16.

42. For an extensive examination of the advisory machinery

and how it was used in three different administrations, see Flash, *Economic Advice and Presidential Leadership.*

43. The extent and growth of this network and of the Council's activities are covered in some detail in the CEA's annual report on its activities, a report that is included as an appendix in the Council's *Annual Report:* January 1962, pp. 195–200; January 1963, pp. 153–165; January 1964, pp. 191–201; January 1965, pp. 171–182; January 1966, pp. 195–203.

44. *Twentieth Anniversary of the Employment Act of 1946,* p. 82.

CHAPTER II: The Promise of Modern Economic Policy

1. Employment Act of 1946, sec. 2.

2. This interpretation of the act's objectives was explicitly endorsed by President Johnson in the January 1965 *Economic Report,* pp. 3–5.

3. Employment Act of 1946, sec. 3. Leon Keyserling was referring to these provisions in 1954 when he said that "the Council should reinstate the earlier practice of projecting, in quantitative terms, *needed* levels of employment, production, and purchasing power. It must do this, to obey the law." *The Employment Act, Past and Future: A Tenth Anniversary Symposium,* Gerhard Colm, ed. (Washington, D.C.: National Planning Association, 1956), p. 71.

4. Kennedy-Heller news conference, Palm Beach, Florida, December 23, 1960, *The New York Times,* December 24, 1960.

5. Keyserling pointed the way in 1954 when he said: "The commitment of the Employment Act to full employment economics, rather than to countercyclical economics, has hardly been noted by most economists, and yet it represents a profoundly valuable and virile shift in mood and emphasis. Here is a unique opportunity for leadership by the CEA." *The Employment Act, Past and Future,* p. 70.

6. In its January 1962 *Annual Report,* the Council, after noting that "careful analyses at the Council and elsewhere . . . lend no

support to the view that frictional and structural unemployment is a rising proportion of the labor force," went on to say that "it would be wholly wrong, however, to conclude that improvement in the structure of the labor market is not both possible and of high importance." And it urged the early adoption of further programs for vocational training and retraining, relocation of displaced workers, and better information on job vacancies. Its thinking on these subjects was set out more fully in its January 1964 *Annual Report,* ch. iii, "The Promise and Problems of Technological Change," and Appendix A, "Testimony of the Council of Economic Advisers Before the Subcommittee on Employment and Manpower of the Senate Committee on Labor and Public Welfare, October 28, 1963."

7. Early in 1961 our calculations showed a gap of nearly $50 billion between the economy's potential of some $550 billion and its actual rate of just over $500 billion of GNP. These calculations are updated and reported regularly in the CEA *Annual Reports,* beginning in January 1962.

8. *Annual Report* (January 1962), p. 142.

9. Although "fiscal drag" is often used generically to describe the retarding effect of any full-employment surplus, its use in the narrower technical sense refers to the automatic growth in potential revenues arising out of the growth in potential GNP.

10. Charles J. Schultze presented the concept of the full-employment surplus in *Current Economic Situation and Short-Run Outlook,* Hearings Before the Joint Economic Committee, Congress of the United States, 86th Cong., 2nd Sess., December 7 and 8, 1960 (Washington, D.C.: G.P.O., 1960), pp. 114–122. The concept was analyzed in some detail both in the Council's January 1962 *Annual Report* (pp. 78–84) and in the testimony of the CEA before the Subcommittee on Fiscal Policy of the Joint Economic Committee, July 20, 1965.

11. The issues involved in the choice between discretionary and automatic stabilizing action, together with the case for the former, are examined in my article, "C.E.D.'s Stabilizing Budget Policy After Ten Years," *American Economic Review* 47:634–651 (September 1957).

12. These figures are based on an analysis presented by the

CEA in its testimony before the Subcommittee on Fiscal Policy. Data used to update them were drawn from the monthly *Survey of Current Business*, Department of Commerce.

13. *January 1963 Economic Report of the President*, Hearings Before the Joint Economic Committee, Congress of the United States, 88th Cong., 1st Sess. (Washington, D.C.: G.P.O., 1963), part 1, p. 8. In these hearings the CEA analyzed and charted in some detail the expected stimulus of the tax cut through the workings of the consumption multiplier and investment responses.

14. Dexter M. Keezer, "Business and Government — Do They Speak the Same Language?" *Saturday Review*, March 5, 1966, p. 23.

15. Arthur Okun's analysis was presented to the American Statistical Association on September 10, 1965, in a paper entitled "Measuring the Impact of the 1964 Tax Reduction." His calculations show that, in the absence of the tax cut, GNP for the second quarter of 1965 would have been $24½ billion below its actual level. His analysis projected an annual increment of $36 billion of GNP as the ultimate payoff on the 1964 tax cut.

16. Sources for the following data were the "Economic Indicators" prepared for the Joint Economic Committee by the Council of Economic Advisers; the Bureau of Labor Statistics, *Labor Review*; and the Department of Commerce, *Survey of Current Business* and *Business Cycle Indicators*. All of these are monthly publications, available from the Government Printing Office, Washington, D.C.

17. These figures differ from those on page 45 which are year-to-year comparisons for 1960 and 1965.

18. Remarks of President John F. Kennedy, Yale University, June 11, 1962.

19. Burns' fears that success and consensus may "spoil the Presidency" are expressed in *Presidential Government: The Crucible of Leadership* (Boston: Houghton Mifflin, 1965).

20. *Economic Report* (January 1966), p. 20.

21. This expected advance followed a strong year-to-year rise of 5.9 percent in real GNP from 1964 to 1965 and a remarkable jump of 7.5 percent between the fourth quarters of 1964 and 1965.

22. J. A. Livingston, "Business Outlook: LBJ Has Become Economic Factor," *Minneapolis Tribune*, April 10, 1966. In his

column, Livingston attributes to the *American Banker* the reference to President Johnson as a "major economic force."

23. According to the Minnesota poll, one of the best of the regional polls, 67 percent of those interviewed in May expected a tax increase (though it should be added that 63 percent thought it "would not be in the best interests of the country"). *Minneapolis Sunday Tribune*, May 29, 1966.

24. If one adds in the transfer payments out of the largely self-financed social security and other trust funds, that is, if one uses the cash budget basis, the percentage stands at about 19 percent for both years. Although the cash budget is superior in measuring economic impact, the administrative budget gives a better picture of the size of Federal programs financed, not by the beneficiaries themselves, but by general-purpose taxes.

25. *Economic Report* (January 1966), p. 18.

26. See the *Economic Report* (January 1962), pp. 17–21, where President Kennedy asked for standby authority for temporary tax cuts, capital improvements speed-up, and unemployment compensation increases in the face of recession. President Johnson's proposal was made in his *Economic Report* (January 1965), p. 11.

27. *Economic Report* (January 1965), p. 10.

28. John Kenneth Galbraith, "Economic Policy Since 1945: The Nature of Success," Salomon Lecture, New York University, November 4, 1965, pp. 26–27 (mimeographed).

29. *Technology and the American Economy*, Report of the National Commission on Technology, Automation, and Economic Progress (Washington, D.C.: G.P.O., February 1966), I, 48.

30. *Technology and the American Economy*, I, 46–47.

31. Walter W. Heller, "The Economic Outlook for State-Local Finance," in *Proceedings of the National Governors' Conference 1965* (Chicago: National Governors' Conference, 1965), p. 51. The term "half-finished society" comes from the title of an article by Edward K. Faltermayer in *Fortune*, March 1965, p. 96.

32. "Remarks of the Honorable Douglas Dillon, Secretary of the Treasury," *Proceedings of a Symposium on Federal Taxation* (New York: American Bankers Association, 1965).

33. June 21, 1965 (*The New York Times*, June 22, 1965).

34. *Minneapolis Tribune*, February 20, 1966.

CHAPTER III: Strengthening the Fiscal Base of Our Federalism

1. L. Laszlo Ecker-Racz, "Federal-State Fiscal Imbalance: The Dilemma," *The Tax Executive* 17:281–289 (July 1965).

2. Joseph D. Tydings, "The Last Chance for the States," *Harper's Magazine*, March 1966, p. 71.

3. Remarks of Richard C. Goodwin to visiting foreign students, July 20, 1965, p. 4 (White House press release).

4. For an insightful discussion, see Max Ways, " 'Creative Federalism' and the Great Society," *Fortune*, January 1966, especially p. 224.

5. Senator Edward M. Kennedy, Address to the National Conference of State Legislative Leaders, San Juan, Puerto Rico, November 13, 1965, p. 2 (mimeographed). The dramatic story of North Carolina's efforts and accomplishments in dealing with the problem of poverty and the crisis in education are described by Governor Terry Sanford in *But What About The People?* (New York: Harper & Row, 1966).

6. Trevor Armbrister, in his article "The Octopus in the State House," *Saturday Evening Post*, February 12, 1966, pp. 25–29, 70–80, presents the seamier side of the story of state government; but even he sees a "vast process of change" going on under pressure from the Supreme Court.

7. One of the most telling defenses of federalism is presented by George C. S. Benson in "Values of Decentralized Government," in his *Essays on Federalism* (Claremont Men's College: Institute for Studies in Federalism, 1961), pp. 5–16. An illuminating discussion of the development of the federal system is provided by James A. Maxwell in the first chapter of *Financing State and Local Governments* (Washington, D.C.: The Brookings Institution, 1965), pp. 10–32. On the Federal idea and the role of the states, see Nelson A. Rockefeller, *The Future of Federalism* (Cambridge, Mass.: Harvard University Press, 1962), especially pp. 6–15.

8. L. L. Ecker-Racz, "Fiscal Crisis in an Affluent Society," in *City Problems of 1966*, The Annual Proceedings of the United

States Conference of Mayors (Washington, D.C., 1966), pp. 103–109.

9. Revenue elasticity — the response of tax yields to growth in GNP and income — of state and local taxes has been the subject of numerous recent studies, especially in connection with state-local fiscal projections. For a useful discussion of state tax elasticities, together with extensive citations of studies on this subject, see the report of the Advisory Commission on Intergovernmental Relations, *Federal-State Coordination of Personal Income Taxes* (Washington, D.C.: G.P.O., October 1965), pp. 40–45. See also Robert Harris, *Income and Sales Taxes: The 1970 Outlook for States and Localities* (Chicago: The Council of State Governments, January 1966), especially pp. 17 and 42. The most comprehensive summary of revenue elasticities of state and local taxes is in Selma J. Mushkin and Gabrielle C. Lupo, "Project '70: Projecting the State-Local Sector," George Washington University State-Local Finances Project (Washington, D.C., March 1966), especially p. 29 (mimeographed). (This paper is to be published in the *Review of Economics and Statistics*.)

10. The revenue and expenditure data for Federal, state, and local governments in this chapter are taken from the various financial compendia of the Bureau of the Census, Governments Division — especially its annual compendium of governmental finances — and from the annual budgets of the Federal government (Washington, D.C.: G.P.O.). See also Maxwell, *Financing State and Local Governments*, for useful bibliographical notes on statistical sources, pp. 263–265.

11. The $2 billion figure somewhat overstates the increase because it does not allow for any rise in productivity in the state-local use of the goods and services purchased. For a refined examination of the price factor in state-local spending, see Selma J. Mushkin and Gabrielle Lupo, "Is There a Conservative Bias in State-Local Sector Expenditure Projections?" George Washington University State-Local Finances Project (Washington, D.C., July 1, 1966) (mimeographed).

12. "Strengthening the States' Tax Base," a statement presented by Governor Orville L. Freeman at the Governor's Conference, San Juan, Puerto Rico, August 4, 1959, p. 4 (mimeographed).

In July 1966 New York City found that it had to pay an interest rate of over 4.6 percent on its bonds, nearly 50 percent more than the 3.1 percent it had paid in April 1965 and the highest rate paid since 1932. The Federal government shared this woe in issuing a note late in July at 5 1/4 percent, the highest rate it had paid in 45 years.

13. The picture for total government receipts on a national-income-accounts basis is similar: in 1946 Federal receipts were 18.7 percent, and state-local receipts 5.9 percent, of GNP. By 1964 the Federal share had dropped slightly to 18.2 percent, while the state-local share rose to 9.3 percent. It will be noted that total taxes in 1964 were about 22 percent of GNP, total receipts, 27.5 percent.

14. John Shannon, "Recent Developments on the State Personal Income Tax Front," Fact Sheet 2 (Washington, D.C.: Advisory Commission on Intergovernmental Relations, November 1965), p. 15 (mimeographed).

15. Joseph A. Pechman, "Financing State and Local Government," *Proceedings of a Symposium on Federal Taxation* (New York: American Bankers Association, 1965), p. 76.

16. Dick Netzer, "State-Local Finance in the Next Decade," unpublished manuscript for the Committee for Economic Development (Washington, D.C., August 1965). Netzer's figures are for fiscal year 1970. His projected receipts of $111 billion include $16.5 billion of Federal aid and $12 billion of new long-term debt issues.

17. Mushkin and Lupo, "Project '70," p. 46. Their projections are for calendar 1970. They use a 5.7 percent annual rate of growth in GNP.

18. From the Bureau of the Census, *Governmental Finances in 1964.*

19. Advisory Commission on Intergovernmental Relations, *Measures of State and Local Fiscal Capacity and Tax Effort* (Washington, D.C.: G.P.O., 1962), pp. 24, 99. The ten states with the highest dependency ratios had an average rank of 41st in per capita income. The ten with the lowest dependency ratios ranked 8th, on the average, in per capita income.

20. Joseph A. Pechman, *Federal Tax Policy* (Washington, D.C.: The Brookings Institution, 1966), pp. 207–208.

21. An interesting examination of the nature of creative fed-

eralism, as viewed from the White House, was presented by Joseph A. Califano, Jr., Special Assistant to the President, in an address before the National Lawyers Club, Washington, D.C., May 19, 1966.

22. The Legislative Reference Service of the Library of Congress has prepared for the Senate Committee on Government Operations a *Catalog of Federal Aids to State and Local Governments* (Washington, D.C.: G.P.O., April 15, 1964, together with supplements of May 17, 1965, and April 6, 1966). This very useful catalog takes over 450 pages to list, index, and summarize the present aid programs.

23. Presidential Economic Issues Statement no. 6, "Strengthening State and Local Government," October 28, 1964 (White House press release).

24. See Harold M. Groves, *Financing Government*, 6 ed. (New York: Holt, Rinehart & Winston, 1964), ch. xx; and Pechman, *Federal Tax Policy*, pp. 225–231 and 306–307 (the latter pages, for further references on this subject).

25. At their annual meeting in 1965, the nation's governors passed a resolution endorsing "study of a proposal to strengthen both the capabilities and the self-reliance of the states by a return of a portion of federal tax revenues each year to the states, without federal controls attached as a condition to the grant . . . ," *Proceedings of the National Governors' Conference 1965*, p. 270. During 1965 numerous bills for revenue sharing were introduced in Congress. Senator Javits (joined by Senators Hartke, Scott, and Mundt) introduced S. 2619, perhaps the most fully developed plan thus far cast in legislative form. It provides for per capita sharing, adjusted both for fiscal effort and for supplemental grants to the poorest states. The companion bill (H.R. 11535) was introduced in the House of Representatives by Representative Reid and was followed by the introduction of identical bills by Representatives Lindsay, Halpern, Ellsworth, Morse, Todd, McDade, Dwyer, and Donahue. The sharing of income tax revenues on the basis of origin was the subject of at least one bill in the Senate and fifteen bills in the House during 1965.

26. Among the many articles discussing per capita revenue sharing, perhaps the most useful is Harvey E. Brazer, "Our Hard-Pressed State and Local Governments," *Challenge* 14 (January-

February 1966), 7–9, 41. Other useful articles include Edwin L. Dale, Jr., "Subsidizing the States," *The New Republic*, November 28, 1964, p. 11; Richard C. Worshop, "Federal-State Revenue Sharing," *Editorial Research Reports* 2:943–960 (December 23, 1964); R. L. Heilbroner, "The Share-the-Tax-Revenue Plan," *The New York Times Magazine*, December 27, 1964, pp. 8, 30–31, 33; Alan Otten and Charles B. Seib, "No-Strings Aid for the States?" *The Reporter*, January 28, 1965, pp. 33–35; "The Muffled Roar Over 'Allowances' for States," *The National Observer*, December 28, 1964. Many of the foregoing articles, together with a number of other items bearing on the revenue-sharing plan, were inserted in the appendix of the *Congressional Record*, August 25, 1965, by Congressman W. E. Brock. They run at intervals from page A-4780 to page A-4816.

27. The estimates used here apply to 1960. They were prepared by W. Irwin Gillespie under the supervision of Richard A. Musgrave, and were published as part of Gillespie's essay, "Effect of Public Expenditures on the Distribution of Income" in *Essays in Fiscal Federalism*, R. A. Musgrave, ed. (Washington, D.C.: The Brookings Institution, 1965). See especially the summary tables on pp. 136 and 162 and the references to other incidence studies on pp. 122–123.

28. For a pioneering expenditure incidence study for a particular state, see O. H. Brownlee, "Estimated Distribution of Minnesota Taxes and Public Expenditure Benefits," *Studies in Economics and Business*, no. 21 (Minneapolis: University of Minnesota, 1960).

29. Pechman, *Federal Tax Policy*, p. 228. The Advisory Commission on Intergovernmental Relations, using a different year and a somewhat different standard of comparison, notes that the relationship between Federal grants and state personal incomes "is barely inverse" and concludes that, looking only at the expenditure side, "the over-all equalization effect of the grants is not yet significant." (*The Role of Equalization in Federal Grants*, Washington, D.C.: G.P.O., 1964, p. 72.) The state-by-state distribution of grants-in-aid fluctuates considerably from year to year. For fiscal 1963, for example, the per capita distribution runs from an average of $63 for the ten highest income states, to $66 for the second ten, $55 for the third, $63 for the fourth, and $50 for the bot-

tom ten. (See the Bureau of the Census, *Governmental Finances in 1963*.)

30. Pechman, "Financing State and Local Government," p. 82.

31. *Congressional Record*, October 11, 1965, p. 25609.

32. See the Commission's report, *Federal-State Coordination of Personal Income Taxes*, especially pp. 14–19.

33. For a comprehensive discussion of tax credits, see James A. Maxwell, "Tax Credits and Intergovernmental Fiscal Relations" (Washington, D.C.: The Brookings Institution, 1962), especially ch. iv. See also my paper, "Deductions and Credits for State Income Taxes," House Committee on Ways and Means, 86th Cong., 1st Sess., *Tax Revision Compendium: Compendium of Papers on Broadening the Tax Base*, vol. 1 (Washington, D.C.: G.P.O., 1959), pp. 419–433.

34. Shannon, "Recent Developments on the State Personal Income Tax Front."

35. S. 2619, Sec. 4 (b).

36. Alan L. Otten, "Governors Make Good Impression," *Wall Street Journal*, July 30, 1965, p. 12. Speaking of American state legislatures, *The Economist* concludes that "a profound change is beginning to sweep through them and interest in their potentialities is reviving" (July 30, 1966).

Index